1. *Ardent Desires*

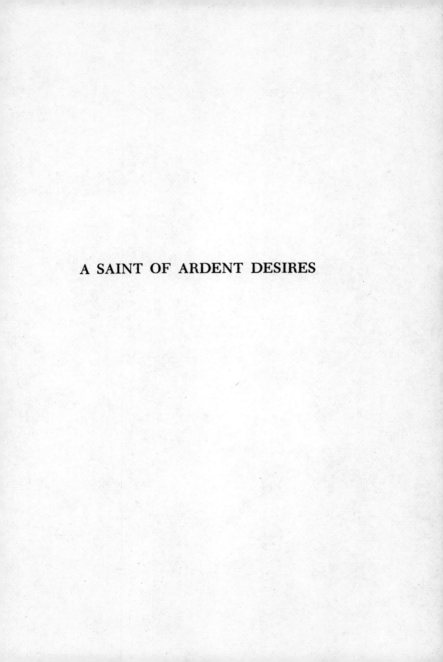

A SAINT OF ARDENT DESIRES

A Saint of

ARDENT DESIRES

MEDITATIONS ON THE VIRTUES OF
ST. THERESE OF LISIEUX

by

Rev. Costanzo J. Antonellis C.S.S.R.

ST. PAUL EDITIONS

IMPRIMI POTEST:

JAOCBUS T. CONNOLLY, C.SS.R., J.C.D.

Provincialis, Provinciae Baltimorensis C.SS.R.

die VI Maji 1964

NIHIL OBSTAT:

MICHAEL J. CANTLEY, S.T.L.

Censor Deputatus

Bruklyni die XXI Aprilis 1964

IMPRIMATUR:

BRYAN JOSEPHUS McENTEGART, D.D.

Episcopus Bruklyniensis

Bruklyni die XXI Aprilis 1964

Library of Congress Catalog Card Number: 65-17556

COPYRIGHT, 1965, by the *Daughters of St. Paul*

Printed in U.S.A. by the *Daughters of St. Paul*
50 St. Paul's Ave., Jamaica Plain, Boston, Mass. 02130

CONTENTS

CONTENTS

Dedicated to my mother and father,

Carmela and Umberto Antonellis.

PROLOGUE

Many and varied works have been published concerning St. Therese of Lisieux. The most delightful writings are those she herself penned in her immortal Autobiography and in her letters. These reveal the wondrous gifts that God so lavishly bestowed on His chosen little one.

Those devout souls who wish to imitate the Little Flower do best by lovingly and attentively reading her writings. All other works are as meditations on what she has written, making it simpler to gather more good from what the Saint has left us.

The purpose of this book is to draw a soul to the imitation of St. Therese, and thus give the good God many little victims of Divine Love. The words of the Saint are used most frequently, for they carry a sacred unction and persuasive force.

The spirituality of the Little Flower is only one type of spirituality. The Church allows many other types to fit the specific demands of individual souls.

The Little Flower is the ninth child of Louis Joseph Stanislaus Martin and Zelie Guerin. She was born on January 2, 1873, at Alencon, France. On January 4, she was baptized in the church of Notre Dame. The saintly mother of the Saint died when Marie Francoise Therese Martin was still a small child. Shortly afterwards, the Martin family moved to Lisieux. That was in 1877.

While still in her teens, Therese entered the austere Order of Carmel, at Lisieux. There, she was known as Sister Therese of the Child Jesus and of the Holy Face. She died at the age of 24. It was on Thursday, September 30, 1897.

On the fourteenth of August, 1921, Pope Benedict XV promulgated the Decree of Heroism of the Venerable Servant of God. On February 11, 1923, Pope Pius XI promulgated the Decree of Approbation of Miracles, presented for the Beatification of Sister Therese. And on the seventeenth of May, 1925, the Solemn Canonization of God's little one took place in the Basilica of St. Peter at Rome.

CostanzO J. AntonellIS, C.SS.R.

PART I

Meditations

on the

Virtues

of

St. Therese

THE DESIRE FOR PERFECTION

"You know, O my God, that I have never desired else but to love You alone. I seek no other glory. Your love has gone before me from my infancy. It has grown with my growth, and now it is an abyss whose depths I cannot sound." (p. 201)*

A burning desire for perfection is the first means that you must adopt to become a saint and give yourself wholly to the good God. And what is perfection? Perfection is love of God. And perfect love of God is the complete union of your will with God's. When you love one deeply and tenderly, you unite your will with that of the beloved, so that your wills are as one. The more you desire to unite your will with the Will of God, the greater will be your perfection. St. Therese of the Child Jesus was a saint of ardent desires. From the tender age of infancy, her heart turned to God. She knew that

* This and all succeeding quotations are taken from *Sainte Therese de l'enfant Jesus*. Histoire D'Une Ame ecrite par elle meme, First French Edition.

she was loved by Him, and desired to love Him with all her strength. She was only two years of age when she heard friends talking of her sister, Pauline. She understood that Pauline was going to be a nun so that she might love God as perfectly as possible. And although she did not quite know what it meant, she decided that she would be a nun, too. It was the desire to love God still more that drew her to the Divine Spouse of Virgins. How good God was to St. Therese, to draw her so gently to Himself from the dawn of reason.

God is good to you, too, and wills that you approach Him with ardent desires. St. Alphonsus Mary de Liguori says that "holy desires are the blessed wings with which the saints burst every worldly tie, and fly to the mountain of perfection, where they find that peace which the world cannot give." By ardent desires, you reach the summit of the mountain of the love of God. And in the embrace of love, peace fills the soul. Through those desires, you find strength to overcome all difficulties. Pains and suffering become light. So ardently did the Little Flower desire perfection, that she once exclaimed: "Now I have no other desire if it is not to love Jesus even to folly. Yes, it is love alone that draws me. I no longer desire either suffering or death, although both are dear to me. For a long time, I have called upon them as messengers of joy. I possessed suffering and I thought I touched the shore of heaven! I have believed from my most tender youth, that the Little Flower would be gathered in the springtime. Today, it is self-abandonment that guides me. I have no other compass. I know not how to ask with eagerness, except the perfect accomplishment of the Will of God in my soul." (p. 145)

Our dear Saint desired nothing else than to do the Will of God in all perfection. Full sweet is the way of Love! It is true. One may fall and be unfaithful to grace. But Love knows how to profit by everything. Love quickly consumes what is displeasing to God, and leaves in the heart only a deep and humble peace. Love urges us on to do the Will of God. And as a reward, the soul has a deep and humble peace. Oh, how the heart aches for this! You should beg God, in His tender mercy, to clasp you to His sweet embrace.

What great heights of sanctity you could obtain, if only you desire it. But you will never arrive at perfection, unless you ardently desire to become a saint. If you desire something earnestly enough, you will use all the means in your power to attain it. You will not be careless about the goal you have in view. You will have it written in your heart and in your mind. You will not rest until you have achieved what you have longed for. Half-way measures will not satisfy the longings of your soul.

There was a Canaanite woman, whose daughter was grievously troubled by a devil. She ardently desired the cure of her daughter. When Jesus was near, she cried out to Him: "Have pity on me, O Lord, Son of David! My daughter is sorely beset by a devil." But Christ was silent. She continued to cry after Our Lord, imploring mercy. She so upset the disciples that they begged Him to send her away. Turning to the woman, Christ said: "I was not sent except to the lost sheep of the house of Israel." But the poor woman came and adored Him pleading: "Lord, help me!" Christ seemed to spurn her, for He answered: "It is not fair to take the children's bread and to cast it to the dogs." But the mother would not be denied. She replied: "Yes, Lord; for even the dogs eat of the crumbs that fall from their masters' table." Then Jesus answered and said to her: "O woman, great is thy faith! Let it be done to thee as thou wilt." And her daughter was healed from that moment. (Matthew 4:21) This mother earnestly desired the cure of her daughter. Nothing deterred her from her goal. Even rebukes did not deter her. In your striving for perfection, the same persistency of this woman must be imitated.

There is a charming incident in the life of our beloved Saint, that illustrates how fully she desired perfection. At that time, she was about three years of age. Leonie, who no doubt thought herself too big to play with dolls, brought a basket filled with clothes, pretty pieces of stuff, and other trifles on which her doll was laid, to Celine and Therese. "Here you are, my little sisters, choose whatever you want!" Celine looked at it, and took a woolen ball. After thinking about it for a minute, Therese put out her hand saying "I choose everything!" And she carried off both doll and basket without more ado. In later years, the Little Flower spoke of this, and said: "This incident of my childhood is as it were a resume of my whole life. Later on, when perfection was presented to me, I understood that to become a saint, it would be necessary to suffer much, to always seek what was more perfect, and to forget oneself. I understood that in holiness, the degrees are numerous, that each soul is free to respond to the advances of Our Savior, to do little or much for His love. In a word, to choose between the sacrifices that He asks. Then, as in the days of my childhood, I cried out: My God, I choose everything. I will not be a saint by halves. I am not afraid to suffer for You. I fear only one thing, and that is to keep my own will. Take it, for I choose all that You will!" (p. 15)

St. Alphonsus, the great Redemptorist, states: "Whosoever, through diffidence of attaining sanctity, does not ardently desire to become a saint, will never arrive at perfection." A man who desires to provide his family with a comfortable home, with food and clothing, must work. But if through dislike of fatigue and difficulties, he shirks his responsibilities, he will never advance a single step towards his wished-for goal. His wife and children will be in want, or have only the bare necessities of life. And he who finds the path of holiness too rugged to walk on, will seek other paths. He will be satisfied with a lukewarm existence, and run the risk of eternal misery. For it is a teaching of the Saints, that he who does not desire, and does not strenuously try, always to advance in holiness, will go backward in the path of virtue. A Christian who seeks to remain stationary in the path of virtue, is like a man who is in a boat on a rapid river, and striving to keep the boat always in the same position. If the boat is not continually worked against the current, it will be carried away in the opposite direction, and, consequently, without continual exertion, its station cannot be maintained. If you do not wish to advance in virtue, you must fail. You must either go forward and advance in the love of God, or go backward and rush headlong into sin.

God usually confers His outstanding favors on those who thirst for His love. Once, St. Aloysius appeared in a vision to St. Mary Magdalene de Pazzi, and said to her: "My eminent sanctity was the fruit of an ardent desire, which I cherished during my life, of loving God as much as He deserved to be loved. And being unable to love Him with that infinite love which He merits, I suffered a continual martyrdom of love, for which I am now raised to that transcendent glory which I enjoy."

The life of a good Christian is one continuous longing after perfection. He longs to unite his will with the Divine Will. Perfect love of God is so obtained. Once you have tasted how sweet it is to love God, you will desire nothing more.

In seeking to become saints, you must not rest. Of this, St. Paul assures you, when he said: " Do you not know that those who run in the race, all indeed run, but one receives the prize? So run as to obtain it." (1 Cor. 9:24) God wills that we become saints: "This is the will of God, your sanctification." (1 Thess. 4:3) St. Therese well understood that we must run continually on the way of perfection. In her beautiful meditation, she exclaimed: "But I have not explained all my thoughts on this passage of the Sacred Canticles: Draw me! We will follow you eagerly! (Canticles 1:4) By asking to be drawn, we desire to be intimately united with the object that has captivated our heart. If the fire and iron were endowed with reason, and the iron were to say to the fire: "Draw me!" would that not prove the iron's desire to identify itself with the fire even to sharing its substance? Very well! There you have my prayer exactly. I ask that Jesus draw me within the flames of His love, to unite me so tightly to Himself that He lives and acts within me. I feel that the more the fire of love consumes my heart, the more I shall say: Draw me! And the more also will souls that draw close to mine, run with swiftness in the sweet odor of the Beloved." (p. 202)

Our Lord has said: "No one can come to Me unless the Father who sent Me draw him." (John 6:44) And later He tells us that whosoever seeks shall find, whosoever asks shall receive, that unto him that knocks it shall be opened. And He adds that whatever we ask the Father in His Name, it shall be given us. If you desire the love of God, you must ask for it. You must seek it. You must plead for it.

So ardently did little Therese desire the love of God, that she became a martyr of divine love. Her immense desires overwhelmed her. Mindful of the prayer of Eliseus, who asked the Prophet Elias for his double spirit, she presented herself in spirit to the company of the Angels and Saints. In the ardor of her desires, she cried out: "I am the smallest of creatures. I know my wretchedness. But I also know how much noble and generous hearts love to do good. I beseech you then, O blessed inhabitants of the celestial city, to adopt me as your child. All the glory you will obtain for me will come back to you. Deign to hear my prayer. Obtain for me, I beseech you, double the amount of your love!" And again she prayed: "What I ask for is love. I know only one thing, and that is to love You, O Jesus. I wish to profit by the smallest actions and to do them for love. O my Jesus, I love You. Jesus, Jesus, if so sweet is the desire of love, how delightful must it be to possess love and enjoy it for all eternity!" (p. 217-219)

The desires of our dear Saint were fruitful, for she used the means to acquire sanctity. How often do some souls yearn to become saints. But when it comes to using the means necessary, they have become tepid and sluggard. They assure themselves that they will begin tomorrow. They build up pretexts to cover up their inefficacious desires. "Oh!" they exclaim, "if I could withdraw from activities, I would spend all my time in prayer!" "If only I were a religious, how holy I would become!" "If I didn't have so many things to do, how I would spend my life loving God." But for all their cries, they think of God but little. Seldom do they go to Holy Communion. They attend the Divine Sacrifice with little devotion. They get too weary with even a few minutes prayer. They do not sanctify their works by offering them to God. Of them, Solomon says: "The soul of the sluggard craves in vain, but the diligent soul is amply satisfied." (Prov. 13:4)

That our desires to acquire perfection be efficacious, the means used by St. Therese will inspire us. Those means may be listed as follows:

1. Meditation.

2. Renewal of her resolution to advance in divine love.

3. Holy unrest that urged her on to greater heights of love.

4. Realization of her purpose in life.

5. Renewal of her desires to advance in love.

6. Courage in striving for perfection.

7. Imitation of good examples.

MEDITATION

Little Therese, the beloved child of God,
thought of God almost always. So intimately was she
united to Him in love and thoughts that she once
said: "I attach no importance to my dreams. Besides, they rarely have any meaning. Yet I ask myself just the same, how is it that since I think of the
good God all day, I don't dwell on Him more in my
sleep." (p. 138) Meditation is nothing more than
thinking of God. It is a familiar conversation and
union with God. That our dear Saint did think of
God all the time is evident in her writings. Everything seemed to draw her to God. That God
enlightened her mind and gave her His love, is proof
of the advantages of mental prayer or meditation.

The Little Flower tells us that as a child, she
would have liked to practice mental prayer, but
Marie, her sister, finding her sufficiently devout, only
let her say vocal prayers. A mistress at the Abbey
asked her once what she did on holidays, when she
stayed at home. And she timidly answered that she

25

would hide in a corner of her room, where she could shut herself in with the bed curtains, and then think. "But what do you think about?" said the good religious laughing. "I think about the good God, the swiftness of life, about eternity; in a word, I think!" "Now I know that I was then engaged in true prayer, in which the divine Master sweetly instructed my heart." (p. 57)

All things seemed to lift the soul of Therese to God in ardent desires and acts of love. When she went fishing with her father, and she was but a child, she preferred to sit on the grass some distance away. Then her reflections became really deep, and, without knowing what meditation meant, her soul was absorbed in prayer. Far-off sounds reached her, the murmuring of the wind, sometimes a few uncertain notes of music from a military band in the town a long way off; all this imparted a touch of melancholy to her thoughts. Earth seemed a place of exile, and she dreamed of heaven. On another occasion, when the blue sky became overcast and a storm came on, accompanied by flashes of lightning, she looked about her to lose nothing of the grand sight. "A bolt of lightning fell in a neighboring field, and far from experiencing the least fear, I was delighted. It seemed to me as though the good God was very close to me." (p. 25)

As a child, even the stars in the heavens lifted the Little Flower's heart to God. She used to look at the stars with inexpressible delight. Orion's belt fascinated her especially, for she saw in it a likeness to the letter "T." "Look, Papa, my name is written in Heaven!" Then, not wishing to see this dull earth any longer, she asked her father to lead her, and with her head thrown back, she gazed unweariedly at the starry skies. Just as our dear Saint did, we can look up into the heavens, and see the love of God for us. Or we can look at the crucifix, where our name is written in the hands, the feet, the side, and the head of Christ.

In the Martin household, St. Therese welcomed the prize day. Rewards would be given her, if she did her school work well. And although she was the only competitor, justice was none the less strictly observed, and she never received rewards unless they were well merited. Her heart used to beat with excitement when she heard the decisons, and in the presence of the whole family, received prizes from her father's hand. "It was to me like a picture of Judgment Day!" declares our Saint. (p. 31)

When she was six or seven years old, she saw the sea for the first time. The sight made a deep impression on her. She could not take her eyes off it. Its majesty, and the roar of the waves, all spoke to her soul of the greatness and the power of God. And at the evening hour, when the sun seemed to sink into the vast ocean, leaving behind it a trail of glory, she sat with her sister Pauline, and gazed long on this golden furrow. Pauline told her sister that this was an image of grace illumining the way of faithful souls. Then little Therese pictured her soul as a tiny bark, with a graceful white sail, in the midst of the furrow, and she resolved never to let it withdraw from the sight of Jesus, so that it might sail peacefully and quickly towards the Heavenly Shore. In like manner, we can pray, asking Jesus to draw us as little barks on the ocean of Love.

St. Therese was so delicately attuned to the supernatural, that even a holy picture would suggest many acts of love. At times, her soul was so intimately united to God, that she would gaze on these pictures in a kind of ecstasy. One such holy picture was "The Little Flower of the Divine Prisoner." While looking at it, she offered herself to be Christ's Little Flower. She longed to console Him, to draw as near as possible to the Tabernacle, to be looked on, cared for, and gathered by Him. Cannot we, in like manner, lift our hearts to God? Bruised flowers we may be, yet Jesus loves us tenderly.

Our Saint reflected on spiritual truths, and those inspired her. She tells us: "Then considering that I was born for glory, and searching for the means of attaining it, it was revealed to me interiorly that my glory would never appear before mortals, but that it would consist in becoming a saint. This desire might seem rash, if you consider how imperfect I was, and how I still am, after so many years spent in religion. Yet I feel the same bold confidence of becoming a great saint." (p. 55) We, too, are called to be saints. We must seek the means that will draw us close to the embrace of God. There is no station in life, no matter how lowly, but that one can become a saint in it. A laborer on a construction job; an electrician wiring a building; a mechanic in a garage; the doctor in his office; the school teacher; the newspaper reporter; the housewife and mother—all can become saints in their walk of life. Sanctity is found not only in the parish house and in the monastery and convent. Sanctity is found wherever men are. It remains up to the individual to think of his soul, and to refresh it in the springs of the sweet waters of Divine Love.

Nor is it rash and bold to have confidence that one day you will become a saint. God can, in the twinkling of an eye, fulfill our most ardent desires. It is not on our own strength that we lean. We rest on the arm of God. With Him holding us up on our steps to perfection, we can and will succeed in becoming saints. Becoming a saint is the work of love. Just as our Redemption was the consummation of Love, our becoming saints is the fruit of Love. What will sustain us and give us the fullest confidence, is the fact that we are actually loved by God. This thought alone captivates our hearts, and causes us to yearn for the divine embrace. The words of the Prophet Ezechiel have been fulfilled in us: "I passed by you and saw that you were now old enough for love. So I spread the corner of my cloak over you to cover your nakedness; I swore an oath to you and entered into a covenant with you; you became mine, says the Lord God. Thus you were adorned with gold and silver; your garments were of fine linen, silk and embroidered cloth. Fine flour, honey, and oil were your food. You were exceedingly beautiful with the dignity of a queen." (Ezechiel 16:8-9; 13) God in His mercy, has loved us, and chosen us to be members of the Mystical Body of Christ. He has washed us in the waters of Baptism; clothed us with sanctifying grace; has placed a chain about our neck, that indelible character of Baptism; and He has fed us with fine flour and honey and oil, of the Most Blessed Sacrament. He has made us exceedingly beautiful. How can we help but love God and have confidence that we shall one day become saints?

Little Therese meditated so often on heavenly things, that even in the midst of her school work, she would pause and feel irresistibly drawn to God. For she tells us: "I went on studying, and what is more important, I kept on growing in the love of the good God. On a number of occasions, I had true raptures of love." (p. 87) We may not experience such spiritual delights and consolation. But surely we can accustom ourselves to sweetly and gently lifting our minds to God, even when occupied with many tasks. Soon, it will become a habit, and we will constantly live in the Presence of God. What joy there is in the realization that we are always in the sight of the One Who loves us with an infinite love and desires our love in return. This thought should give us the strength to do all for love of Jesus.

Meditation is possible at all times, for God has made it so that we can be drawn to Him by every creature. Even a pleasure trip can be a source of heavenly inspiration. For the wonders of nature will reveal the goodness of the Creator. So it was with the Little Flower. While on her pilgrimage to Rome, with her father and sisters, she would look out the train window. Sometimes, she was high up the mountain side, while at her feet an unfathomable abyss seemed ready to engulf her. A little later she was passing through a charming village with its cottages and graceful belfry, above which light fleecy clouds floated lazily. Farther on a great lake with its blue waters, so calm and clear, would blend with the glowing splendor of the setting sun. To Therese, this was a foretaste of the wonders of Heaven. She tells us that as she gazed on the works of God thoughts of religious life would come before her, as it really is, with its constraints and daily sacrifices made in secret. She understood how easily one might forget the sublime end of one's vocation, and she thought: "Later on, in the hour of trial, when, as a prisoner of Carmel, I cannot see but a small corner of the sky, I will remember this day. This tableau will give me courage. I will no longer make much of my small interests, when I reflect on the grandeur and power of God. I will love Him alone and will not have the unhappiness of attaching myself to things of straw, now that my heart has experienced what is in store for those who love Him." (p. 97) How well we, too, can do as did our beloved Saint. In the times of trial, we can think of the many good things God has given us, and we will be happy to bear suffering for love of Him.

Once you have accustomed yourself to lifting your thoughts to God, you will do so even in times of pleasant conversation or recreation. Love will press your heart, and in this urgency, you will be drawn into the sweet intimacy of God. A word, a look, a picture, all will be as so many divine arrows of love. Such was the life of Little Therese. To cite an instance of this, we may recall how intently she listened to the story of hypnotism. She was told of the strange phenomena produced by magnetism on persons who surrendered their will to the hypnotiser. Later, she said: "O how much good your conversation did for me yesterday! Oh! How I would love to be hypnotised by Our Lord. That's the first thought I had when I awoke this morning. With what sweetness I surrendered my will to Him! Yes, I want Him to take possession of my faculties in such a manner that I no longer perform human and personal acts, but actions that are all divine, inspired and directed by the Spirit of love." (p. 290)

The Saints have been brought closer to God by the fruits of the field, by flowers, by animals. For all these creatures spoke of the goodness of God. One holy man used to gently tap the flowers in the field, and say: "Do not rebuke me for not loving God enough!" Another would gaze at a ripe peach, and think of the love of God who made this fruit that she might enjoy it. Our beloved Saint also was brought nearer to God by the sight of God's creatures. One day, she took an ear of corn from a sheaf that had been brought to her. It was so laden with grain that it bent on its stalk. After gazing upon it for some time, she said to the Mother Prioress: "Mother, that stalk of wheat is the image of my soul: the good God has loaded it with graces for myself and for the good of others! Ah! I wish always to bend under the abundance of heavenly gifts, acknowledging that they all come from above." (p. 243)

2. *Ardent Desires*

Meditation should come easily to those who love God. In the Second Book of Machabees, a mother exhorts her seven sons to die for God, rather than break His laws. In her words is revealed that she thought of God often, or meditated. Speaking to them, she said: "I know not how you were formed in my womb, for I neither gave you breath, nor soul, nor life, neither did I frame the limbs of every one of you. But the Creator of the world, that formed the nativity of man, and that found out the origin of all, he will restore to you again in his mercy both breath and life, as now you despise yourselves for the sake of his laws." (2 Machabees 7:22-23) When a mother gazes lovingly on her children, the words of the valiant woman can well fill her heart.

The sailor at sea can see the majesty of God in the ocean. A farmer can see the mercy of God in the growth of his crops. The craftsman can see the wisdom of God in the laws that govern his handiwork. All of us, regardless of our walk in life, can see the relationship it has with God, if we but will it. Meditation inflames the heart with love. As Holy David says: " In my thoughts, a fire blazed forth." (Ps. 38:4) If we cannot set aside a definite time to meditate, then we should do so at other times, gently and sweetly lifting our thoughts to God.

St. Therese was inflamed with love of God by meditating on the Sacred Scriptures. Ardent desires and acts of love came spontaneously to her while she read the inspired words. Once while reading the twelfth and thirteenth chapters of the First Epistle to the Corinthians, she read that all cannot become Apostles, Prophets, and Doctors; that the Church is composed of different members, that the eye cannot also be the hand. And she tells us that meditating on the Mystical Body of Holy Church, she could not recognize herself among any of its members as described by St. Paul—rather, she wished to recognize herself in all. Charity provided her with the key to her vocation. She understood that since the Church is a body composed of different members, the noblest and most important of all the organs would not be wanting. She knew that the Church has a heart, that this heart burns with love, and that it is love alone that gives life to its members. She knew that if this love were extinguished, the Apostles would no longer preach the Gospel, and the Martyrs would refuse to shed their blood. She understood that love embraces all vocations, that it is all things, and that it reaches out through all the ages, and to the utmost limits of the earth, because it is eternal. Then, beside herself with joy, she cried out: "O Jesus, my love! At last I have found my vocation! My vocation is love! Yes, I have found my vocation in the bosom of the Church, and it is You, O my God, who has given me this place. In the heart of the Church, my Mother, I will be love! Thus I shall be all things; thus shall my dreams be realized." (p. 216)

By a devout reading and meditation on the Sacred Scriptures, God will be pleased to inflame us with desires and acts of love. The entire Autobiography of St. Therese is enriched with quotations, with brief meditations from the Word of God. To read the life of our dear Saint will give us greater love for the Sacred Scriptures, and for the good God Who has given them to us.

It must be remembered, however, that the advantage of mental prayer consists not so much in meditating as in making acts of love, petitions and resolutions. The progress of a soul does not consist in thinking much of God, but in loving Him ardently. This love is acquired by resolving to do a great deal for Him. St. Francis de Sales used to say that by obtaining the divine love we obtain all graces. For a soul that truly loves God with its whole heart, will of itself, without being admonished by others, abstain from giving Him the smallest displeasure, and will labor to please Him to the best of its ability.

St. Alphonsus says: "The ejaculations that are dearest to God are those of love, of resignation, of oblation of ourselves. Let us endeavor not to per-

form any action without first offering it to God, and
not to allow at the most a quarter of an hour to
pass, in whatever occupations we may find ourselves, without raising the heart to the Lord by some
good act. Moreover, in our leisure time, such as
when we are waiting for a person, or when we walk
in the garden, or are confined to bed by sickness,
let us endeavor to the best of our ability to unite
ourselves to God."

If we imitate St Therese in familiar conversation and union with God, which is meditation, God
will be pleased to inflame us with His divine love.
May the love of God take possession of us.

RENEWAL OF RESOLUTIONS

We should often renew our desires and resolutions to advance in the love of God. If we live as though each day were the beginning of our service to God; or as though this day were the special day of loving God, how much closer we would be in His embrace. St. Therese tells us: "As I grew up, I loved the good God more and more, and I often gave Him my heart, using the method mother had taught me. I forced myself to please Jesus in all my actions, and I was careful never to offend Him." (p. 26) By these words, our beloved Saint tells us that she lived constantly in the sweet Presence of God. She knew that God loved her, and she loved Him in return. Because she often renewed her resolutions to love Jesus, her heart was enkindled with love. And on the occasion of her First Holy Communion, her joy on sacramentally receiving the living Body of Jesus was so intense, so deep, that it could not be restrained. Tears of happiness welled in her eyes and overflowed. All the joy of

Heaven had come down into her heart, and she could not contain it without tears. "Ah! How sweet was the first kiss of Jesus on my soul! Yes, this was a kiss of love! I felt myself loved, and I also said: 'I love You, and I give myself to You forever!' Jesus asked nothing of me, and claimed no sacrifice. For a long time, now, He and little Therese had known and understood one another. That day, our meeting was more than simple recognition, it was perfect union. We were no longer two. Therese had disappeared like a drop of water in the bosom of the ocean. Jesus remained alone. He was the Master, the King." (p. 59) St. Therese had one great wish. It was to love God only, and to find her joy in Him alone. How ardently we should desire the same! Often should we renew our resolutions of loving God with our entire being. For in loving God, we have all. How good it is to kneel before Jesus in the Most Blessed Sacrament, and there to renew our resolutions to love Him and to become saints for the love we bear Him. From the tabernacle, Christ will console us with His love and give us strength to carry out our resolutions. The burning sparks of love which He will cast into our souls, will make us lose sight of all earthly things, and to yearn for His enfolding embrace.

Before Christ in the Most Blessed Sacrament, what resolutions are made; what strength to fulfill our ardent desires. Jesus will manifest Himself to our hearts. Doubt will no longer be possible. Faith and hope will give place to love. A foretaste of Heaven will be granted us. The practice of virtue will gradually become sweet and natural to us. Each grace faithfully received will bring many others. St. Therese, speaking on the mercy of God, revealed how her resolutions were fulfilled. "How merciful is the path down which the divine Master has always lead me! He has never had me desire anything without giving it to me. I wished that my face, like the face of Jesus, should be 'one of those from whom men hide their faces, spurned and held in no esteem.' (Isaias 53:3) I thirsted to suffer and be forgotten." (p. 121)

In making resolutions that will help us to become saints, we must have absolute confidence in God. We must not measure God's Omnipotence by our own narrow thoughts. God is so good, that He wills to give us more than we ask for. He is infinite in His love. We cannot ask too much of His love. On this matter, St. Therese says: "Often, the Lord is content with the desire to work for His glory. And you know, my Mother, that my desires have been very great!" (p. 162) She no longer had any desire but to love Jesus till she died. She had surrendered herself wholly to Jesus, and He was free to do with her whatsoever He pleased. Her one interior occupation was to unite herself more and more closely to God, knowing that the rest would be given to her over and above. And she tells us that "my hope has never been deceived." Put yourself in the arms of Jesus. Open your heart to Him. Tell Him your resolutions, and He will do the rest. "Just as a torrent draws after it into the depths of the sea all that it meets in its path, even so, O my Jesus, the soul plunges into the shoreless ocean of Your love, draws to itself every treasure." (p. 200)

One resolution that we must make is to imitate our Blessed Lord in suffering. We must fulfill in our bodies what is lacking of suffering in the Mystical Body of Christ. St. Therese teaches: "I had to pass through many trials before attaining the shore of peace, before tasting the delicious fruits of total abandonment and perfect love." (p. 43)

The devout Thomas à Kempis speaks thus: "Jesus hath now many lovers of His heavenly kingdom, but few bearers of His cross. He hath many that are desirous of consolations, but few of tribulations. He finds many companions of His table, but few of His abstinence. All desire to rejoice with Him, but few are willing to endure anything for His sake. Many follow Jesus to the breaking of bread, but few to drink of the chalice of His Cross. Many reverence

His miracles, but few follow the ignominy of His Cross. Many love Jesus as long as they receive some consolations from Him. But if Jesus hide himself and leave them for a little while, they are either murmuring or fall into excessive dejection. But they that love Jesus for Jesus' sake, and not for the sake of some consolation of their own, bless Him no less in tribulation and anguish of heart than the greatest consolation." (IMITATION OF CHRIST)

Meditating on the words of Our Lord: "And I appoint to you a kingdom, even as My Father has appointed to Me," (Luke 22:29) little Therese explains, "that is to say, I will store up crosses and trials for you; thus you will become worthy to possess My kingdom. If you wish to sit by His side, you must drink the chalice that He Himself drank." (p. 104) "Yes, I can say that not only in the matters I am now writing about, but also in other trials still more acute, suffering opened its arms to me from my entrance and I have embraced it with love. When you want to attain an end, you must use the means necessary. Jesus made it known to me that He would give me souls through the cross. Moreover, the more I met the cross, the more my love of suffering increased. For five years, such was my way of life. But only I was aware of this. And there you have precisely the unknown flower that I wished to offer Jesus, that flower whose perfume would be breathed forth only on the side of heaven." (p. 118)

In her resolutions to advance in the love of God, St. Therese was greatly attracted towards penance. But many times, because of bad health, she was not able to fulfill her wishes. And so she endeavored to practice little hidden virtues, such as folding mantles forgotten by the Sisters. But she constantly mortified her self-love, and this did her more good than bodily penance would have done.

Our Saint was not free of heart-aches. How surprised many would be to read her words, saying: "My soul has known many kinds of crosses. I have suffered very much here below! In my childhood, I suffered with sorrow. Today, I taste all bitter fruits with peace and joy." (p. 156) For many, the thought of death is terrifying. They shrink from suffering and from the Judgment to come. How differently St. Therese thought of suffering. On one occasion, she visited the Altar of Repose throughout Holy Thursday night. When she returned to her cell at midnight, she had an unusual experience. Scarcely had her head laid on the pillow, when she felt a hot stream rise on her lips. She thought she was going to die, and she adds, "and my heart nearly broke with joy." But since she had already put out her lamp, she morti fied her curiosity until the morning, and slept in peace. At five o'clock when it was time to get up, she remembered at once that she had some good news to learn, and going to the window, found, as she had expected, that her handkerchief was soaked with blood. To St. Therese, this was like the first call of Jesus, "like a sweet, distant murmur, heralding His joyful approach." (p. 157)

How good it is to think of the words of St. Therese. "For is there any greater joy than to suffer for Your love? The more intense is the suffering, and the more it is hidden from the eyes of creatures, the more it causes You to smile, O my God." (p. 160) "When you expect only suffering, you are rather surprised by the least joy. And the suffering itself becomes the greatest of joys when you seek it as a precious treasure." (p. 164) "True love feeds on sacrifices. The more the soul denies itself natural satisfactions, the stronger and more detached does love become." (p. 182) "Ah! It is prayer and sacrifice that make up my whole strength. They are my invisible weapons. They, better than words, can move hearts." (p. 186)

On the day of her religious profession, St. Therese cried out: "O Jesus, I ask for peace alone! Peace, and above all, love, boundless, limitless love! My Jesus, for love of You may I die a martyr. Give me martyrdom of heart or of body. Ah! Rather give me them both!" (p. 134) That God did give her martyrdom of soul, we know. God, in His mercy, let the infinite tenderness of His divine love flow into the soul of St. Therese. And since she could not love Him with all the love He merits to be loved with, her soul suffered a true martyrdom. Martyrdom of body, our dear Saint also had—not in the same sense of the Martyrs who shed their blood for Christ, but she so lovingly embraced all suffering in imitation of Christ Crucified, that in this sense, she is a martyr of body.

To those who think the offering of oneself as a victim of divine love to be one of ease and consolation, St. Therese has this to say: "To offer yourself as a victim of Love, means to offer yourself to all His anguishes." (p. 224)

On one occasion, someone remarked to St. Therese: "They say that you never suffered very much." Then smiling, and pointing out a glass filled with a sparkling red potion, she said: "Do you see that little glass? You might think that it was filled with a delicious liquor. Actually, I taste nothing more bitter. Well, that is the image of my life. To the eyes of others, it is clothed in radiant colors. It seems to them that I drink exquisite liquor. Yet, it is bitterness! I say bitterness, and yet my life has not been bitter, for I have known how to make all bitterness my joy and sweetness." (p. 235)

Once, when some were distressed in seeing St. Therese in pain, she replied: "Oh! Do not get upset about me. I have reached such a stage that I can no longer suffer, because all suffering is sweet to me. Besides, you are quite wrong in thinking about what sorrows are in store for me. It is like meddling with creation! We who run in the way of love must never torment ourselves about anything. If I did not suffer from moment to moment, it would be impossible for me to keep my patience. But I see only the present moment, I forget the past, and I am careful not to envisage the future. If one at times despairs, it is because one thinks of the past or the future. In the meantime, pray for me. Oftentimes, when I beg God to come to my help, it is just then that I feel the most abandoned." (p. 235)

With the Prophet Job, St. Therese could say: "Slay me though He might, I will wait for Him." (Job 13:15) On this quotation, our beloved Saint tells us: "But the word of Job has not entered my heart in vain. I confess that it has taken me a long time to establish myself at this degree of abandonment. Now I am there. The Lord has taken me and placed me there." (p. 236)

There is yet another resolution that should be renewed often, and that is detachment from all human affections. God has given us a heart to love with, and the heart cannot exist without some kind

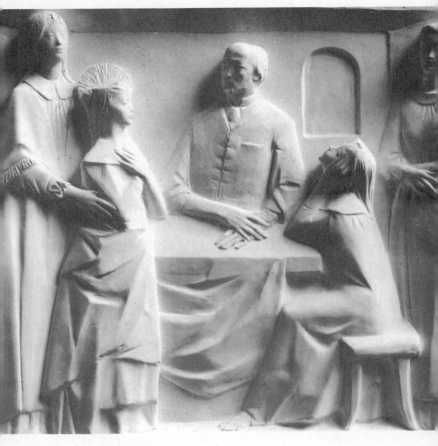

St. Therese and Her Family—E. Giaroli

"He who loves father or mother more than Me
is not worthy of Me." (Matt. 10:37)

of love. But the heart that is too closely united with human loves, so that it forsakes God for those loves, runs serious risk for its salvation. When friendships and affections draw us to God, then they are good. However, Our Blessed Lord warns us that there is danger in all loves that do not lead to Him. "He who loves father or mother more than me is not worthy of Me; and he who loves son or daughter more than Me is not worthy of Me. And he who does not take up his cross and follow Me, is not worthy of Me. He who finds his life will lose it, and he who loses his life for My sake, will find it." (Matt. 10:37) And again: "If anyone comes to Me and does not hate his father and mother, and wife and children, and brothers and sisters, yes, and even his own life, he cannot be My disciple. So, therefore, every one of you who does not renounce all that he possesses, cannot be My disciple." (Luke 14:26-33) Does this mean, then, that we cannot love a dear friend, our brothers, sisters and parents? Are we not commanded to love our neighbors? We must love our neighbor as ourselves. Love will fill the heart. But it must be that love which will not take us away from God, or will not wound our souls in any way. As St. Augustine says: "Love God and do what you will." For if you truly love God, all other loves will be a manifestation of your love for Him.

But we must keep in mind that our souls may easily be led astray by self-deception. Creatures made by God are visible to the eye and good to behold; their possession is oftentimes desired. But God is a pure Spirit, and cannot be seen. Although He possesses all perfection, all beauty and is infinitely good, our frail human nature will not always tend to the embrace of God.

St. Therese loved her family dearly. She was of an affectionate nature, wishing to be loved and returning love for love. But God, wishing to possess her heart entirely, caused her to find only bitterness in human friendships. Later, when in the convent, with her sisters, she practiced heroic detachment towards them, even though she loved them ardently. While at school, as a child, she observed that some of the girls were very devoted to the teachers. She tried to imitate them, but never succeeded in winning any special favor. When writing her life, she says: "O happy failure! From what great evils you have spared me! How I thank the Lord that He has made me find nothing but bitterness in friends on earth! With a heart such as mine, I would have allowed my wings to be clipped; then how could I "fly away and be at rest?" (Ps. 54:7) How can a heart given up to human affection be intimately united with God? It seems to me that it is impossible. I have seen many souls seduced by a false light, cast

themselves into it, and like poor moths, burn their
wings. And then wounded, they return to Jesus, that
divine fire that burns without consuming." (p. 63)
Here it must be noted that our dear Saint is speaking of those affections that lead away from God.
It is so easy to go astray in the seductive paths
of human friendships and affections. But, without
doubt, to a soul somewhat advanced in virtue, the
sweetness offered by human loves is mingled
with bitterness, and the immense void of its desires
cannot be filled by them.

The devout Thomas à Kempis says that "the
love of things created is deceitful and inconstant;
the love of Jesus is faithful and enduring. He that
clingeth to the creature shall fall with its falling.
He that embraceth Jesus shall be firmly rooted.
Love Him, and keep Him for thy friend, Who, when
all forsake, will not leave thee, nor suffer thee to
perish finally. Sooner or later thou must be separat-
ed from all, whether thou wilt or no." (Ch 7) How
true are those words. The embrace of creatures is
like that of a shadow, which shall one time disappear.

When Little Therese was a postulant, she keenly desired to talk with her sister. This natural desire
for one she loved so spiritually, she overcame. But
it caused her such a struggle interiorly, that she was
obliged to hurry past her cell, and hold on to the

banisters to keep herself from turning back. She could think of many pretexts for yielding to her desires, but she did not use them. Later on, when her soul was strengthened by detachment from all human loves, she was able to say: "I no longer feel the need to deny myself the consolations of the heart, for my heart is fixed in God. Because I have loved Him above all, my love has grown little by little so that I can give to those dear to Him a tenderness incomparably more profound than if my love were self-centered and barren." (p. 182)

God desires our whole heart and all our love. Let us consecrate our whole soul and all our affections to Him. Despite our faults, God still calls us to love Him: "Thou shalt love the Lord thy God with thy whole heart." Let us obey Him and love Him completely, utterly. We should pray that we may be consumed with that love.*

*May I point out that all material things and human relationships are good in themselves, and can and ought to be used for our spiritual advancement. St. Therese's spirit of detachment was a special gift from God, one He sometimes gives to select souls for reasons known only to Himself. The Saint's language may sound strange and unfeeling and almost beyond understanding, unless this fact is kept in mind. What we ought to try to imitate is her spirit of detachment within the limits of the grace and the vocation that God has given us.

HOLY UNREST

A soul that loves God is never at rest. The more love that the soul receives from the good God, the more love it desires. The thirst of love is never slaked. An ardent desire for more love is had with each increase of divine love. On one occasion, Little Therese saw a picture of Our Lord on the Cross. It had half slipped out of her prayer-book. Her heart was torn with grief to see the Precious Blood falling to the ground, with no one to treasure it. From that day on, the cry of the dying Savior, "I thirst!" sounded incessantly in her heart, and enkindled therein a zeal she had hitherto not known. She felt herself consumed with thirst for souls, and she longed at any cost to snatch sinners from the everlasting flames of hell. She seemed to hear Our Lord whispering to her as He did to the Samaritan woman: "Give me to drink!" "It was a true exchange of love," says our dear Saint.

"Upon souls, I poured the Blood of Jesus. To Jesus, I offered those same souls refreshed with the

dew of Calvary. In this way, I thought to quench
His thirst. But the more I gave Him to drink, the
more the thirst of my poor soul increased, and I accepted this ardent thirst as a most delicious reward."
(p. 77)

How good it is to know that God loves us, and
desires our love, that He gives us His Heart. In the
olden days, pure and spotless holocausts alone were
acceptable to the omnipotent God. His justice was
appeased by the most perfect sacrifices. Great and
perfect souls offered themselves up to be victims
of holocaust to the justice of God. But how often
was the most beautiful attribute of God neglected.
God is love. Yet how few souls offered themselves
to be victims of holocaust to the love of God.
Once a soul knows that God loves it with an
infinite love, it does not rest until it rests in the
Eternal Home of love in Heaven. Speaking on God's
love, St. Therese tells us: "Yes, that love may be
fully satisfied, it must stoop even to nothingness
and transform that nothingness into fire. O my God,
I know that 'Love is repaid by love alone.' (St. John
of the Cross) And so I sought and found the means
to give solace to my heart, by returning love for
love." (p. 217)

Our dear Saint so often speaks of the mercy of
God. The word mercy melted her heart with love,
for she fully understood what it meant. The word

mercy, is taken from the Latin: misericordia. Taken apart, the word is made up of these parts: miseris, cor, dare: to give one's heart to the wretched. Saint Therese, in her humility, considered herself one of God's least creatures. And because she was one of "the most wretched," God delighted to stoop down to give her His Heart. And she exclaimed that if God could find a soul weaker than hers, He would work still greater wonders within it. "O Jesus, would that I could tell all little souls about Your ineffable condescension! I feel that if You could find a soul more feeble than mine, which is hardly possible, You would be pleased to load it with still greater favors, provided she abandoned herself to Your infinite mercy with full confidence." (p. 221)

The manifestation of holy unrest, or yearning for greater love of God is had in many ways. The soul is humble. It acknowledges that of itself it is nothing, that if it has any virtue or any good, all this comes from the goodness of God. When St. Therese began her Autobiography, she explained: "If a little flower could talk, it seems to me that she would simply tell what the good God has done for her, without trying to hide her gifts. Under the pretext of humility, she would not say that she was ugly and without scent, that the sun had dulled her brilliance, that the storms had bruised her stalk, when she knew very well that it was just the other way around. The little flower that is now going to tell her story rejoices that she can make known the wholly undeserved graciousness of Jesus towards her. She acknowledges that there was nothing in her capable of drawing the divine favors on her, and that it was His divine mercy alone that has heaped blessings on her." (p. 7)

Saint Therese was fully conscious of the majesty of God, and His infinite goodness. Her littleness before God, caused her to refer to herself now as a 'tiny bark'; again as a 'grain of sand'; later on, as a 'little brush.' When asked before her death how they should pray to her in Heaven, St. Therese made this answer: "You will call me 'Little Therese'— petite Therese." At other times, she called herself a 'Little Flower.' In such ways, did she acknowledge God's goodness to her. She remained ever humble. She was as nothing before God, and marveled at the infinite love He bore her.

Holy unrest is seen by the self-abandonment of the soul to God. The soul gives itself over entirely to the will of the beloved. It wishes to make itself one with the lover. To abandon ourselves entirely to God, and by so doing love Him perfectly, our will must be one with His. In joys and in sorrows, in contempt and in praise, the soul must see the Will of God offering all things for its eternal happiness. It realizes that whatever befalls it is either directly willed by God or permitted by God. Just as He causes the flowers in the field to grow, and vests them with great beauty; just as He causes the sparrow to fall; just as all the laws governing the world and the entire universe, are all manifestations of the Will of God in nature and a manifestation of His love, even so, whatever befalls a soul is permitted or done because of the Will of God. And the Will of God is one and the same as the Love of God.

By abandoning itself to the Will of God, the soul is in peace. And peace is had when the body is subjected to the soul, and the soul to God. Or, it may be said that we possess peace when we have harmony between our body and soul; harmony between ourselves and our neighbors; and with God and ourselves. It is a sweet ordering of things so that all is subjected to the Will of God. Being subject to the Will of God, is to be ruled by Love. And what greater delight can a soul have than to be governed by love? To be overwhelmed by an infinite love! When we look upon all things that happen to us through the eyes of love, everything works good unto us.

But this self-abandonment to the Will of God is not easy in the beginning. When death takes away a beloved friend or dear relative, the agony of parting may hide the love that has done this thing.

Mental and physical suffering, too, clouds the mercy of God. And, yet, we know that in all things the Love of God is manifest. To advance in love, that divine unrest press us on to greater acts of love of God, the soul must abandon itself to God in whatever may come upon it.

St. Therese always desired to love God alone. It was her only ambition. So completely had she abandoned herself to the Will of God, that all things were sweet to her, even the most bitter suffering. Speaking of her love, she spoke thus to Jesus: "Love attracts love. Mine bounds towards You, and would wish to fill to the brim the abyss that draws her. But alas! It is but a drop of dew lost in the Ocean! To love You as You love me, I would have to borrow Your own love. Then alone would I find rest. O my Jesus, it seems to me that You could not crown with more love any soul than You have heaped upon me. That is why I dare to ask that You love those You have given me, just as You have loved me." (p. 201) By uniting our will with the Will of Jesus, we make His love our love! The Heart of Jesus will reign within us!

Holy unrest is made known by the ardor with which one desires to receive the living Body of Christ in Holy Communion. The soul is not satisfied with one embrace of Jesus. It pants for love. It thirsts for love. The hour in which the soul can have Christ as its Guest is the most delightful one of the day. And throughout the day, the soul turns sweetly to Christ present in the Most Blessed Sacrament, and words of endearment are uttered, words welcoming Him to the soul, tender exchanges of love. The soul laments that not all love Jesus as He ought to be loved. It grieves that He is left so much alone. It longs to console His Heart ever burning with love towards men and so little loved in return. The soul thinks that there are so many altars where Christ is so abandoned; there are so many places where Christ rests, with hardly a sign of recognition by even those who should love Him most. All this causes the soul to have unrest. It yearns to make up to Him all that is lacking in the love that should be given Him.

Speaking of her First Holy Communion Day, our beloved Saint said: "My happiness was undisturbed. Nothing could ruffle my inward peace. At last, night brought an end to this beautiful evening. The brightest days are followed by nightfall. That day alone, of the first, the eternal communion in our heavenly home, shall be without a setting sun. The next day, my eyes were covered with a certain veil of melancholy. The beautiful clothes, the gifts I had received, could not satisfy my heart! From now on, only Jesus could content me, and I sighed for that blessed moment when I could receive Him for the second time." (p. 60) St. Therese tells us that after the second visit of Our Lord in Holy Communion, she longed for nothing else but to receive Him. And since in those days frequent Holy Communion was not permitted, and only the most devout were permitted to go once or twice a week to receive Jesus in Communion, the feast days on which Christ came to her soul seemed far apart.

It might be imagined that the Little Flower had transports of love when Christ came sacramentally within her soul. We do know that at times she experienced raptures of love, but this was not often. "What will I say about my acts of thanksgiving at such times and always! There is no other time that I am less consoled! But isn't this natural, since I desire the visit of our Lord not for my happiness but only to please Him?" (p. 140)

How great was her joy, as sacristan at Carmel, in being allowed to touch the Sacred Vessels and prepare the altar linen on which the Body of Our Lord would rest. She felt that she must increase in fervor, and she often recalled those words addressed to deacons at their ordinations: "Be you holy, you who carry the Vessels of the Lord."

Her love for Jesus had taken such possession of her, that she was able to say: "For a long time, I no longer belong to myself. I am given over complete-

ly to Jesus. He is, then, fully at liberty to do with me
whatever He wishes. He offered me the gift of complete banishment, and asked if I would consent to
drink this chalice. I immediately wanted to take hold
of it, but He, withdrawing His hand, showed me
that He is content with the acceptance alone."
(p. 164) Her reception of Jesus in Holy Communion gave her that love which caused her to
abandon herself entirely to the Will of the Beloved.

For a soul to have holy unrest, it must possess
love for Mary, the Mother of Jesus. She is the Mother of Fair Love. Through her we have received the
greatest of gifts, God Himself. If we desire to grow
in love of God, we must grow in love for Mary.
Since childhood, Little Therese loved Our Blessed
Mother dearly. And on the occasion of her first Confession when she was exhorted by the priest to a tender devotion towards Our Lady, she said: "I made
the resolution to redouble my love for the Blessed
Virgin, who already held a very large place in my
heart." (p. 27)

On the day of her First Holy Communion,
St. Therese was chosen to read the act of Consecra-
tion to Our Lady for herself and her companions.
With all her heart, she consecrated herself to the
Blessed Virgin Mary, and asked the Mother of God
to watch over her. She seemed to look lovingly down
on the Little Flower. St. Therese loved Mary deeply.

"Had she not herself, on the morning of the 8th of May, placed her Jesus, 'a flower of Saron, a lily of the field' (Cant. 2:1) in the chalice of my soul." (p. 60) Has not Mary planted that same Flower within our own souls? Oh, let us cry out to her: "Oh, sweetest Mary, often have you planted the Flower of Love within my withering soul. Oh, may I love this Flower and be the earth to nourish it!"

One of the strongest means of aquiring holy unrest which urges us to greater union with God, is the imitation of Christ in His sufferings. In the life of our beloved Saint, suffering was one of the means she used to become a saint. She begged for the grace to be a martyr for Jesus, and felt in her soul that her prayer was answered. We cannot love what we do not know. And until we fully grasp how much Jesus has suffered for love of us, we cannot really love Him with all our hearts. St. Therese thought often of the Passion of Christ. In her intense longing to be like Him in all things, she said: "The death of love that I yearn for, is that of Jesus upon the cross." (p. 255) In His infinite love, God heard her prayer. For what greater grace can there be than to imitate Christ, especially in His Sacred Passion? From the heights of Heaven, God touched His little one. The darkness of death gradually enveloped her, and her soul was steeped in bitter anguish. Her soul completely given over to love and suffering, she

clasped the crucifix in her failing hands. The sweat
of death lay on her brow. In her suffering, she turned
and asked the Prioress: "Mother, is it not the agony?
Am I not about to die?" "Yes, my child, it is the
agony. But perhaps Jesus wills that it be prolonged
for some hours." "Ah, very well, then . . . very well. . .
Oh! I would not want to suffer less!" Then looking
at her crucifix, she said: "Oh! I love Him! My God,
I . . . love You!" (p. 254) May we not ask that
God in His goodness permit us to imitate Him
in His Passion? For suffer we must. But if it be with
and in and for Christ, how sweet will it not be!

What we should fear is to be satisfied with the
spiritual state we are in. Should that happen, it is a
sign that we have stopped advancing in the love of
God. It may even be a sign that we are withdrawing
from Him. God is worthy of infinite love. If a tiny,
finite heart does not yearn for full possession of this
abyss of Love, it is because it has blinded itself to
the beauty of God, the inexhaustible richness and
delight of the Divine Majesty. Poor heart of clay! It
will soon be drawn by perishable loves. From this
danger, we should beg the grace of persevering in
the love of God. And it is through Mary, our sweet
Mother, that we will obtain this grace.

We are all called by God to become saints. And
so it is that we all must have a holy unrest that will
goad us on to greater acts of love of God. It makes

no difference what our walk in life may be. The Will of God must still be embraced. Love must be loved. An aid to this is to pray that God will give us the grace to live in His Presence all the day long; the grace to understand that we must turn our hearts sweetly and gently to Him throughout the day. Doing this, we will long to love Him more and more. And with each increase of divine love, our souls will thirst for still more love.

How strange it is that we must be urged to love Love Itself! We are so easily led to love creatures for reflecting some of the goodness of God. But the Divine Son, the Source of all loveliness, is not ardently desired!

On reading the life of St. Therese, our hearts are stirred by the holy unrest that fills its pages. A Saint of ardent desires, she seemed to be like a divine spark, caught in the flames of an infinite fire of love. How good God is to give us such an example to imitate. Surely He will listen to her prayer: "I beg of You, my Jesus, to look down upon a vast number of little souls. I beg of You to choose in this world, a legion of little victims, worthy of Your love!" (Her Life p. 222)

May God grant us the grace to be little souls and victims of His divine love, as was our beloved Sister. May the love that God will grant us enable us to cry out in accents of deepest love, as did Little

Therese: "O Word Divine! O my Savior! You are the Eagle I love Who lures me. You are the One that hurling Yourself towards this land of exile, has willed to suffer and die, so that You might carry off souls and plunge them into the heart of the Holy Trinity, love's eternal home! You are the One Who scaling the heights to the inaccessible light, remains hidden in this valley of tears under the appearance of a little, white host. And You do this so that You might nourish me with Your substance! O Jesus! Let me tell You that You have loved me even to folly. And what do You will in the face of such folly, but that my heart soar towards You? How can my confidence in You have any limits?" (p. 220)

REALIZATION OF HER PURPOSE IN LIFE

How salutary it is to think on the fact that we are in this world to become saints. This thought stirs us from our lethargy. It goads us on to advance continually in holiness. It gives us courage to overcome all obstacles. Little Therese, on this matter, says: "Then considering that I was born for glory, and searching for the means of attaining it, it was revealed to me interiorly that my glory would never appear before mortals, but that it would consist in becoming a saint." (p. 55) Our dear Saint thought on life, and knew that we have not here an eternal city. We are made to know, love and serve God; and as a reward for loving God, to be happy with Him forever in Heaven. But unfortunately, the world knows well how to combine its pleasures with the service of God. How little it thinks of death! And yet death has come to many people, young, rich and happy. Recall to mind the delightful places where they lived, and ask yourself where they are now. What profit do they derive today from the beautiful houses and grounds where they enjoyed all the good things of life? "All is vanity besides loving God and serving Him alone." (IMITATION 1 ch. 1, 3) Once you have found your vocation in life, use it to full advantage to sanctify yourself. That is what St. Therese did. "From illusions, the good God in His mercy, has preserved me. I found the religious life what I thought it would be. No sacrifice surprises me. And yet you know that in my first steps I came across more thorns than roses." (p. 117)

It is so easy to make excuses for not advancing in the love of God. It seems as though some divorce the idea of sanctity from their vocation in life. Whereas both should be in unison, they are placed apart. A state in life, whether it be the married state, the religious, or single state, is chosen as means that will best help us to attain holiness, that will lead us to a closer union with God. And, yet, how often do some look with envy at the life of a religious, saying to themselves: "It is easy for Sister to become a saint. Oh, I should have entered the convent." Some will talk about the priesthood, saying that a priest by his very calling must become holy. Or a religious brother is so sheltered from worries and worldly problems, that sanctity is within easy reach for him. Now while it is true that the priesthood and religious life offer many advantages,

St. Therese Petitions Pope Leo XIII To Enter Carmel—E. Giaroli

"Oh Word Divine! Oh my Savior! You are the Eagle
I love Who lures me."

and, all things being equal, are the highest vocations because they more directly lead to God, all walks of life can be a means of salvation, of sainthood.

Nor is great, worldly knowledge necessary to become a saint. A poor, illiterate can just as easily love God as the greatest scholar. Sometimes those least thought of in the eyes of the world, are those dearest to God. Speaking on this subject, St. Therese says: "I understood that the love of our Lord is revealed just as much in the simple soul that does not resist His graces, as well as in the most learned. As a matter of fact, it is characteristic of love to humble itself. If all souls resembled those of the holy Doctors who illuminate the Church, it seems that the good God would not be stooping low enough in going just to them. But He created the infant that can do no more than utter feeble cries. He created the poor savage that has nothing but the natural law to guide him. It is exactly to such hearts that He deigns to lower Himself. These are the flowers of the field whose simplicity ravishes Him. And by this action whereby He stoops so low, the Lord shows His Infinite grandeur. Just as the sun shines at the same time on the cedar and the little flower, the same divine Star shines in a special way on every soul, great or small, and all respond to His goodness, just as in nature the seasons of the year are so disposed that on the appointed day they cause the humblest daisy to blossom." (p. 5)

When we come across difficulties and sorrows in our state of life, it is easy to indulge in self-pity. Instead of using them as means to sanctify ourselves, we groan under the burden, and seek an escape. But in all this, we hardly think of the Will of God. It may happen that we complain that we should not have those trials and crosses. And again we think of the religious as having a life of bliss, with no suffering or hardship to ruffle their way of life. However, it must be remembered that all walks of life must share in the Cross of Jesus. We are all members of the Mystical Body of Christ, and as such, must fill up in our own members the suffering lacking to it. Christ our Head has suffered; we, the members, must also suffer. But if we keep before our eyes the fact that we are on this earth to become saints, suffering itself will turn into joy.

When St. Therese entered Carmel, she did not lead a life free of toil and heartaches. For some, it is surprising to hear her say: "I found the religious life what I thought it would be. No sacrifice surprises me. And yet you know that in my first steps I came across more thorns than roses." (p.117)

When our dear Saint began her religious life as a sweet maiden of fifteen years, she left the comforts and affections of home. Although her soul was at peace and her happiness was great, she was immediately launched into the sea of sorrows. First of all, she experienced spiritual dryness; and this is none other than finding no delight or consolation in spiritual things. When a soul goes through this agony, its only peace is to know that such is the Will of the Beloved. And love being strong, the soul is willing to bear this cross. But when you add trials from those you live with, the heart is in greater distress. It seems like an abandonment both by God and by men. Such was the experience of St. Therese.

The superior found fault with her wherever she met her. On one occasion, when she had left a cobweb in the cloister, before the whole community, the superior said: "You can easily see that our cloisters are swept by a fifteen-year-old child! Do go and clean away that spider's web, and be more careful in the future." (p. 117) On the rare occasions that she spent an hour with the superior for spiritual direction, the superior seemed to be scolding her nearly all the time, and what pained Therese most of all was that she did not see how to correct her faults. One example was her slow ways and want of thoroughness in her duties, faults which the superior was careful to point out.

While Little Therese was a postulant, the Mistress used to send her every afternoon at half-past four to weed the garden. This was a real penance for her, the more so because she was sure to meet the superior on the way. Once she remarked: "But really, this child does absolutely nothing! What kind of novice is this anyhow, that you have to send out for a walk every day?" (p. 118) And it was in this way that she was invariably dealt with. Later, speaking of these trials, our beloved Saint says: "Yes, I can say that not only in the matters I am now writing about, but also in other trials still more acute, suffering opened its arms to me from my entrance and I have embaced it with love." (p.118)

What is your reaction when you find sorrows in your state of life? Have you a kindred spirit to St. Therese?

While St. Therese was in Carmel, her father suffered a stroke of paralysis, and mental affliction. This caused inexpressible grief to the Little Flower. As we know, she was suffering from spiritual dryness and from misunderstandings in the cloister of Carmel. Now that her father was stricken, she could not go to him for she could not leave the cloister. But despite her trials, she was able to write: "My desire for suffering was filled to the brim. Yet my attraction for it did not lessen. Thus my soul would soon share in the trials of my heart. Spiritual dryness increased. I found no consolation either in heaven or on earth. And yet in the midst of these waters of tribulation that I had called for with all my strength, I was the happiest of creatures." (p. 127)

It must not be imagined that St. Therese found the companionship of these Sisters in Carmel always pleasant and agreeable. She had natural dislikes. But for love of God, she overcame her repugnances and showed kindnesses and sisterly love to each. One particular case is worthy of note, since our dear Saint spoke at some length on it.

She tells us that there was a Sister St. Peter at Carmel. Shortly before this nun became quite bedridden, it was necessary every evening at ten minutes to six for someone to leave meditation and take her to the refectory. It cost St. Therese a good deal to offer her services, for she knew the difficulty, or, I should say, the impossibility of pleasing the poor invalid. But she did not want to miss such a good opportunity for she recalled Our Lord's words: "Amen I say to you, as long as you did it for one of these, the least of my brethren, you did it for me." (Matthew 25:40) She therefore humbly offered her aid. It was with difficulty that she induced the old nun to accept it, but after considerable persuasion, she succeeded. Every evening, she would shake her hour-glass, and St. Therese understood that she meant: "Let us go!" Summoning up all her courage, she rose and the ceremony began. First of all, Sister

St. Peter's stool had to be moved and carried in a particular way, and on no account must there be any hurry. The solemn procession then began. St. Therese had to follow the good sister, supporting her by the belt. She did so as gently as possible, but if by some mischance she stumbled, she imagined that Little Therese did not have a firm hold, and that she was going to fall. "Ah! My God! you are going too fast. I'm going to break my bones." When St. Therese tried to lead her more gently and slowly, she said: "But follow me, won't you! I can't feel your hand. You're letting me go and I'm going to fall. Ah! I was right when I said you were too young to accompany me." (p. 193) When they reached the refectory, St. Therese had to settle the poor invalid in her place, taking great pains not to hurt her. Then she had to turn back her sleeves, always according to her own special rubric. After that, she was allowed to go.

Now one cold, winter evening, St. Therese was occupied in the lowly work just mentioned, when she suddenly heard in the distance, the harmonious strains of music outside the convent walls. She pictured a drawing room, brilliantly lighted and decorated, and richly furnished. Young ladies, elegantly dressed, exchanged a thousand compliments, as is the way of the world. "Then my eyes turned towards the poor invalid I was taking care of. Instead of a melody, I heard from time to time, her plaintif sighs. Instead of gilded walls, I saw the bricks of our austere cloister, hardly visible in the dim light. This contrast moved me sweetly. The Lord enlightened my soul with rays of truth that overshadowed the darksome glitter of worldly pleasures. I would not have exchanged the ten minutes I used in performing my act of charity, to enjoy a thousand years of those worldly festivals." (p. 194)

In all she did, St. Therese kept before her eyes the fact that she was in the world to love God in this life and to be with Him forever in heaven. For that reason, even the most disagreeable tasks became sweet to her, for she accepted them all to draw herself closer to the God of Love. However, St. Therese tells us: "I did not always practice charity with these transports of joy. But in the beginning of my religious life, Jesus wished me to experience how sweet it is to see Him in the souls of His spouses. And so when I led my sister St. Peter, it was with so much love, that I could not do better if I were guiding Our Lord Himself." (p. 195)

If only we could imitate this charity of St. Therese! How we should pray that in whatever tasks assigned to us in our state in life, we act as did our beloved Saint. How close we would then be to God! How perfectly we would fulfill the reason for our being in this world!

St. Therese was very human. There were many things that upset her in the beginning. For example, the rattling of a Rosary so annoyed her that she was bathed in perspiration, and had a difficult time in not showing her displeasure. Gradually, she was able to accept this little trial. And she goes on to say: "I made up my mind to listen carefully, as though this had been the most ravishing concert, and my prayer, which was not one of quiet, was pasted in offering this music to Jesus." (p. 196) At another time, when she worked in the laundry, the Sister opposite her, while washing handkerchiefs, repeatedly splashed dirty water on her face. St. Therese's first impulse was to show the offender she would be glad if she would behave a little more quietly. But the next minute, she thought how foolish it would be to refuse the treasures God offered her so generously. She made special efforts to welcome this shower of dirty water. "You see that I am a very little soul that cannot offer the good God anything but very little things. And yet it often happens that I let these little sacrifices escape that give such peace to the heart. But that does not discourage me. I put up with having a little less peace and try to be more vigilant the next time." (p. 196)

St. Therese had mastered herself so well, that she was able to say: "When I suffer much pain, when painful and disagreeable things happen to me, instead of a sorrowful air, I reply with a smile. In the beginning I did not always succeed. But now it is a habit that I am very happy to have acquired." (p. 247)

Because the Little Flower kept the fact that she was in this world to become a saint constantly before her, she strove to advance in sanctity. There are so many things that will befall us, not to our liking. But if in all things, the loving Hand of God is seen, directing all things for our sanctification, how gladly would we embrace them.

It sometimes happens that we resolve to love God with all our heart, with all our mind, with all our strength, with all our soul. We truly desire to become saints. But within a short space of time, our fervor dwindles, and we give ourselves up to former habits of tepidity. For that reason, once we have resolved to become saints, we must renew holy desires often. We must recall to mind why God made us. Even in the midst of trials and heartaches, we must continue to love God, knowing that His tender mercy is constantly with us.

St. Therese found joy where we often find sorrow. Being overlooked and ignored by creatures became to her a source of delight. On one occasion when she was suffering more than usual, St. Therese overheard a Sister in the kitchen talking about her. "Sister Therese of the Infant Jesus is going to die soon. And I ask myself, actually what can our Mother Prioress say about her after her death, for this little sister, lovable as she is, has surely done nothing that would be worth the trouble to write about." (p. 234) Those words, unknowingly spoken near St. Therese, did not upset her. She had long ago given herself entirely over to the love of God, and it mattered not what others might think of her. And yet, how would we react if others spoke in that way about us? Picture yourself close to death. Your body is racked with pain, and your soul is tortured with spiritual dryness. Then, you hear others say that you will die soon. But your life is so insignificant, that it will be difficult even to say a few words of praise about you. If you did not live entirely for God, these words would crush you.

You might say that St. Therese's faith in God was so strong, that all suffering became light. She foresaw the joys of Heaven and they bore her up in all her sorrows. But it was not always so. Before she died, her soul was enveloped in thick darkness, and her temptations against Faith, although always conquered, were there to rob her of her happiness at the thought of death. "Were it not for this trial," she would say, "I think I should die of joy at the prospect of soon leaving this earth." Once, her temptations against Faith were so strong, that she said: "Last night I was seized with true anguish and my darkness increased. I do not know what accursed voice said to me: 'Are you sure that you are loved by God? Did He come and tell you? It isn't the opinion of creatures that will justify you before Him.'" (p. 237) But the Little Flower did not lose her confidence in God. "The good God has always come to my aid: He has helped me and led me by the hand from my tenderest infancy. I rely upon Him. My suffering can reach the extreme limits, but I am sure that He will never abandon me." (p. 237)

Isn't it true that at times the terrible fear that pierced the soul of St. Therese fills us with dread? In severe trials, have we not asked ourselves: "Are you certain God loves you? Has He told you so Himself?" Unless we keep in mind that God is directing us safely on a sure path to Heaven, we cannot know peace. By means of the words in her "Story of a Soul," St. Therese teaches us that we are on this earth to know, love and serve God. Though ignored by this world during her lifetime, she glorified God during her life, and even now continues to glorify Him. She fulfilled God's purpose in creating her.

Are we fulfilling God's purpose in creating us?

COURAGE

In striving to become saints, we will become aware of our many imperfections. The light of the grace of God will illumine our soul, and we will see our faults clearly. It may happen that from time to time, we will fail in doing good. There is danger, then, of giving up the desire to become holy. We may be tempted to become mediocre, with the false notion that we can remain at a certain spiritual level, and somehow enter Heaven. St. Alphonsus says: "If you have said that you have already attained sufficient perfection, you are lost. For not to advance in the way of God is to go back."

There was a time when St. Therese was much upset about her faults. Even if she offended someone unintentionally, she fretted and made herself ill. But gradually, she overcame this weakness, and was able to say: "The good God has given me the grace never to be cast down by any passing event. When I remember how I used to be, my soul overflows with gratitude. Through the favors I have received from heaven, there has been such a change in me, that you would not know me as the same person." (p. 70)

There are people who make the worst of everything. We should do just the opposite. See the good side of things, and even if our portion be suffering, without a glimmer of solace, we should still make it our joy. In this, our dear Saint gives us the example. "Now, thinking of the pains, the sufferings that await me, I get up all the more joyous and full of courage, for I see more opportunities of bearing witness to my love of Jesus, and, since I am a mother of souls, to earn a living for my children. Then I kiss my crucifix, place it gently on my pillow, and while I am getting dressed I say: 'My Jesus, you have worked enough, wept enough during your thirty-three years on this poor earth. Today, take your rest. It is my turn to do battle and to suffer.' " (p. 278)

We know that it was ever the desire of the Little Flower to become a saint. But she always felt, in comparing herself with the Saints, that she was as far removed from them as the grain of sand, which the passer-by tramples underfoot, is remote from the mountain whose summit is lost in the clouds. Instead of being discouraged, she concluded that God would not inspire desires which could not be realized. We may aspire to sanctity in spite of our

littleness. Reflecting on her littleness, our beloved
Saint says. "For me to become great is impossible.
I must put up with myself just as I am with my
numberless imperfections. But I want to find a
means of going to heaven that is a little way, very
direct and very short, a way that is entirely new. We
are in an age of inventions. Now it is no longer
necessary to put up with the inconvenience of
walking upstairs. In the homes of the rich, an elevator takes its place quite nicely. As to myself, I
would also find an elevator that will lift me up even
to Jesus, for I am too little to climb the rough stair-
way of perfection. Then in the Holy Bible, I sought
for a suggestion of an elevator, the object of my desire, and I read these words that came forth from
the mouth of Eternal Wisdom: 'Let whoever is simple turn in here.' (Prov. 9:4) I then drew close to
God, knowing that I had found what I had been
looking for. Wanting to know what He would do to
one who is 'simple' I continued my hunt, and this
is what I found: 'As nurslings you shall be carried
in her arms, and fondled in her lap. As a mother
comforts her son, so will I comfort you.'" (Isaias
66:12-13) (p. 154)

Never was she consoled by words more tender
and sweet. In happiness, St. Therese cried out:
"The elevator that must lift me up even to heaven
are Your arms, O Jesus! For that reason I have no

need of growing up. On the contrary, I must remain little, and I must become so more and more. O God, You have gone beyond my expectation." (p. 154)

With this same daring confidence of St. Therese, we must place ourselves in the arms of Jesus. In that sweet embrace, He will carry us on the way to perfection. Our Divine Savior loved little children. He took them to Himself and kissed them. And with accents of sweetest love He told us to become as little children, so that we might be lovable in His eyes. Oh, how we should desire to be little that we might be so loved by Jesus. St. Therese tells us that while a child is small, all its wants will be provided by the father. But once the child has grown to man's estate, then the father will tell the son to go to work and take care of his own needs. To avoid this in the spiritual life, we must remain always as children, entirely dependent on the care and caresses of Jesus for all our wants.

But it must not be thought that to remain as children we do not have to take an active part in the love affair of salvation. We must act as though all depended on ourselves, but with the knowledge that all our strength comes from God.

On a certain occasion, a nun asked St. Therese if Our Lord were not displeased at the sight of her own many failings. This was her answer: "Be reassured. He whom you have taken for your Spouse certainly has every desirable perfection. But, if I dare say it, at the same time He has a great infirmity. He is blind! And there is a science He does not know: mathematics. These two defects that would be most regrettable lacks in a mortal spouse, render ours infinitely amiable. If it were necessary that He see clearly and knew mathematics, don't you believe that in the presence of our sins, He would cause us to return to our nothingness? But no! His love for us renders Him positively blind. And moreover, understand this. If the greatest sinner on earth were to repent at the moment of death and expire with an act of love, immediately, He would not take into account the number of graces this unfortunate one has abused, He would no longer see all the crimes he has committed. He will only take into account his last prayer, and will take him without delay into the arms of His mercy. But to render Him blind, and to hinder Him from making the slightest addition, it is necessary to take Him through His heart. That is His weak side." (p. 280)

With child-like confidence and love, let us humbly draw close to Jesus. Let us take our places among the imperfect, and look upon ourselves as little souls who at every instant need to be upheld by the goodness of God. From the moment He sees us fully convinced of our nothingness, and hears us call out to Him, He reaches out His hand to us.

Gently, the Little Flower instructs us, saying: "But if we try to do something great, even under the pretext of zeal, He leaves us alone. It is enough, then, to humble ourselves, to bear our imperfections meekly. Therein—for us—is found perfection." (p. 272)

There are times when our faults will distress us, because we fear that we have wounded the Heart of Our Beloved. But it must be remembered that all faults do not pain the Sacred Heart. Sometimes, through human weakness, we commit faults with no intention of hurting Jesus. Once, St. Therese had all kinds of interior trials, for she wished to yield herself entirely to God, to launch her soul in that ocean of confidence and love. But she dared not. She knew that she had faults, and grieved that they might be offending the Sacred Heart. During the general retreat following her profession, she revealed her whole soul to the priest in the confessional. He assured her that Christ was well pleased with her soul. "Oh! how happy I was on hearing those consoling words!" exclaimed St. Therese. "Never had I heard it said that faults could be committed without giving pain to the good God. This assurance filled me with joy. It made me bear patiently the exile of this life. It was also an echo of my intimate thoughts. Yes, for a long time I believed that the Lord is more

Therese's Profession—E. Giaroli

"O Jesus, I ask for peace alone! Peace, and above all,
love, boundless, limitless love!"

tender than a mother, and I have known the depths of more than one mother's heart! I know that a mother is always ready to forgive the little, involuntary faults of her child. How often have I not had this sweet experience! No reproach could have touched me as much as only one caress. I am of such a nature that I shrink from fear. With love, not only do I advance, I fly!" (p. 136)

Oftentimes, St. Therese is thought of as a lovely Saint who did not need great courage and strength to attain sanctity. Her life is read without much concentration on what her words mean. Dom Gueranger states as follows: "In this world there is no fruitfulness without suffering—either physical pain, secret sorrow, or trials known sometimes only to God. When good thoughts and generous resolutions have sprung up in our souls through reading the lives of the Saints, we ought not to content ourselves, as in the case of profane books, with paying a certain tribute of admiration to the genius of their authors—we should rather consider the price which, doubtless, they paid for that supernatural good they have produced."

Today St. Therese has won many hearts and drawn them to the God of Love. But what price did she have to pay? She suffered much for Jesus. And suffering demands great courage.

The Little Flower was naturally proud and impetuous by nature. Instances of this are made known in her autobiography. One day, her mother wanted to see how far Little Therese's pride would go. She was only three years of age, then. "Therese," said she, "if you kiss the ground, I'll give you a penny." In those days, a penny was a fortune, and Little Therese didn't have far to stoop. She was so tiny, that there wasn't much distance between her and the ground. But her pride was up in arms. "Oh! No, mother, I like it better not having the penny." (p. 13)

Two years later during the month of May, 1878, Little Therese stayed at home, while her sisters went to the May devotions. She was too small to go. So every evening, she and the nurse had a little altar at home. St. Therese had arranged it according to her own taste. Everything was small—candlesticks, vases and the rest. One evening, when Therese and the nurse went to their prayers before this altar, she asked the nurse to begin the Memorare, for she was going to light the candles. The nurse tried to begin, and then looked at Therese and burst out laughing. Seeing the precious little candles burning quickly away, the Little Flower begged the nurse to say the Memorare, but again, the silence was broken by bursts of laughter. Then all the Saint's natural good temper deserted her. She got up, dreadfully angry, stamped her foot, and called the nurse a naughty girl. The nurse stopped laughing, and looked at Little Therese in utter astonishment. Too late, she showed Therese two candles she had hidden under her apron. Tears of anger on our dear Saint's face were soon changed to tears of sorrow.

These little stories point out that St. Therese was proud and impulsive. But she had to be told but once what was right, and she would ever afterwards do it. On this, St. Therese says: "But Jesus watched over his little fiancee. He turned to her advantage all her faults, which checked in time, helped her grow in perfection. In fact, just as I had self-love and love of good as well, it was enough to tell me only once: 'You musn't do such a thing' and I no longer had any desire of doing it again." (p. 13) And since St. Therese did all for the love of God, what great spiritual courage she possessed that enabled her to do so.

St. Therese's courage is revealed when she writes: "It seems to me that I had the same disposition that I have today, for even then I had a great command over all my actions. Thus, I had developed the habit of never complaining when what was mine was taken away from me. Also, when I was unjustly accused, I preferred to keep quiet rather than make excuses. "There wasn't any merit in this on my part.

I did it naturally." (p. 16) Here, our dear Saint is speaking of her childhood. This spirit, she kept throughout her lifetime. At Carmel, she strove to be the little servant of her Sisters in religion. In the same spirit of humility, she endeavored to obey all without distinction.

There are many stories that reveal the courage of St. Therese. On a certain occasion, the nuns at Carmel had gathered in the garden to sing a hymn before an altar of the Sacred Heart. St. Therese was already wasted by a fever. She joined the Community, and arriving fully exhausted, she was obliged to sit down. When the hymn began, one of the Sisters made a sign for Therese to stand up. In spite of her fever and great oppression, she got up and remained standing to the end.

The infirmarian thought it good to advise the Little Flower to take a little walk in the garden each day for a quarter of an hour. Perhaps this would strengthen and refreshen her. But it proved otherwise. One afternoon, a Sister, noticing the effort of St. Therese, said: "You would do much better to rest yourself. Under such conditions, your walk doesn't do you any good. You utterly exhaust yourself!" "It is true!" she replied. "But do you know what it is that gives me the strength? Well! I am walking for a missionary. I am thinking that down there, far away, one of them is perhaps exhausted in his apostolic work, and to lessen his fatigue, I offer mine to the good God." (p. 228)

One day, when Little Therese had suffered much in humiliations from one of her companions in religion, a Sister noticed how happy was our dear Saint. She inquired what gave her such great joy, and received the reply: "It is because Sister N. has just been saying disagreeable things to me. Oh! How this pleases me! Now I would like to meet her so that I could smile upon her." (p. 229) And as she was speaking, the Sister in question knocked at the door. The astonished novice could see for herself how courageous and good was St. Therese. Later, St. Therese acknowledged that she "soared so high above all things earthly, that she came from humiliations made stronger." (p. 229)

Often did St. Therese suffer dizziness and headaches. But this did not prevent her from taking part in all the Community acts. She followed all the practices of the austere Rule of the Carmelites, from her entrance at the age of fifteen. Only the fasts were excepted.

The Little Flower used to say that she never did any great penances. That was because she counted as nothing the few that were allowed her. However, on closely reading her autobiography, it is evident that our beloved Saint performed great interior penances. To cite some instances of this, we recall that one day a certain Sister visited Little Therese, who was confined to bed because of physical exhaustion. She noticed that Therese's face was diffused with joy, and sought to know the reason. "It is because the pain is so acute just now," she replied. "I have always forced myself to love suffering and give it a welcome." And still again, when she was asked why she was so cheerful one morning, our beloved Saint answered: "Because of two little crosses. Nothing gives me 'little joys' like 'little crosses.'" At another time, when she was suffering much, she was asked if she had had many trials that day. The Little Flower replied: "Yes, but I love them! I love all the good God sends me!" It might be asked where she obtained this extraordinary courage and strength in the greatest trials. The Saint answered: "Could a little victim of love find what her Spouse sends her, frightful? Each moment, He gives me what I can bear, nothing more. And if the next moment He increases my sufferings, He also increases my strength. However, I could never ask Him to increase my sufferings, for I am too little. They would then become my own sufferings, and it would be necessary that I bear with them all by myself. And I never could do anything by myself." (p. 247)

To obtain courage to advance in holiness, even in the midst of suffering, we can meditate on the words: "Could a little victim of love find what her Spouse sends her, frightful?" Surely, the thought that everything that befalls us is from the hands of our Lover, should spur us on in the road of perfection. as St. Therese teaches: "Ah! I have well experienced it. Joy is not found in the things surrounding us, but resides within the inmost recesses of the soul. One could just as well possess it in the depths of a darksome prison as in a royal palace. Thus, I am happier in Carmel, even in the midst of trials, both interior and exterior, than in the world where nothing was wanting to me, above all, the sweetness of the family hearth." (p. 109)

Before her death, St. Therese gave proof of her words in the manner in which she bore her suffering. She became so weak that she was unable to make the slightest movement without assistance. Even to hear anyone whisper increased her discomfort. Her fever and oppression were so extreme that she could scarcely articulate a single word. And yet, a sweet smile was always on her lips. She did not want to give the Sisters extra trouble, and so wished to be alone during the night. Only two days before her death would she allow anyone to remain with her during the night. On one occasion, the infirmarian came into St. Therese's cell at night, and

found her with hands joined and eyes raised to
Heaven. "Now do tell me what are you doing so?"
she asked. "You should be trying to get to sleep." "I
cannot, Sister, I am suffering too much. And so I
pray." "And what do you tell Jesus?" "I tell Him
nothing. I just love Him." (p. 252)

"Oh! how good God is!" she sometimes exclaimed. "Truly He must be very good to give me
strength to bear all I have to suffer." (p. 218)
The courageousness of our beloved Saint is revealed
in the words, written in pencil with a trembling
hand: "O my God, how good You are to Your little
victim of merciful love! Now even as You join
exterior suffering to the trials of my soul, I cannot
say: 'The breakers of death surged round about me,
the destroying floods overwhelmed me.' (Ps. 17:5)
But in my gratitude I cry: 'Even though I walk in
the dark valley, I fear no evil; for You are at my
side, Lord.' " (Ps. 22:4) (p. 252)

The courage of St. Therese was great, because
her confidence and love of God was great. She had
surrendered herself wholly to Jesus, and He was
free to do with her whatsoever He pleased. Once,
when she was asked, "What do you do, to practice
virtue like this, to be so constantly happy, calm and
at ease with yourself?" She replied: "I have not
always acted so. But ever since the time I no longer
sought myself, I lead the happiest life one could pos-

sibly have." (p. 275) The Little Flower detached her heart from all earthly cares, especially from creatures. She had one only desire left, and that was to love Jesus with her entire being. And because of this, courage to sanctify herself was given her by the Divine Spouse.

In imitation of the Little Flower, let us cling to Jesus with child-like confidence. With complete abandonment to His Will and to His Love, we will obtain that courage to overcome all obstacles in the way to sanctity.

IMITATION OF GOOD EXAMPLE

To become a saint, it is important to imitate the good example of those about us. The kindness of one, the thoughtfulness of another, the spirit of prayer of your neighbor, the zeal for divine worship, the holy simplicity of another, and the various virtues you see exercised in those about you. Holy zeal will prompt you to rival and even excel others in practicing virtues, especially the love of God. People oftentimes seek to surpass one another in riches, honors, and earthly pleasures. We ought to struggle for superiority in humility, patience, meekness, charity, love of contempt, poverty, purity, and obedience. But to succeed in this holy contest, we must perform all our ordinary actions with the intention of pleasing God and of edifying our neighbors that they may sanctify themselves and give greater glory and love to God. It is well to note that just as good example stimulates to virtue, so, too, bad example gives scandal and leads many into the faults which they see every day.

"Ah! How many souls would have attained a high degree of holiness if from the beginning, they had been well directed! I know that God has no need of anyone to accomplish His work of sanctification. But just as He permits a clever gardener to cultivate rare and delicate plants, giving him, for this end, the necessay knowledge, while reserving to Himself the right to make them grow, even so He wills to be helped in the divine cultivation of souls. What would happen if an ignorant gardener did not graft his trees in the right way? If, for example, he did not know the nature of each, and would want roses to blossom on a peach tree?" (p. 88)

The Little Flower's life gives witness to the power of good example on her soul. She tells us that all her life, God was pleased to surround her with affection. Her first recollections were of smiles and tender caresses. God, in His goodness, enlightened the mind of St. Therese, so that she had the use of reason at an earlier age than usual. Her good mother and father often spoke of heavenly things. They taught her of the love of God for souls. They pointed out that God rewarded the good and punished the wicked. All these things made a profound impression on her mind, as is shown in the following incident. Her good parents had spoken of the joys of Heaven, and made it understood that one would have to die before entering this life of happiness. And so on one occasion, she embraced her mother, and while kissing her, said: "Oh, how I wish you would die, dear Mamma!" When she was scolded, she was quite astonished, and answered: "But I want you to go to Heaven, and you say we must die to go there." And in her outburst of affection for her father, she wished him to die, too. With the directness and simplicity of a child, the Little Flower had learned the lessons taught by her dear parents. Mrs. Martin always said morning and night prayers with her children, and this example left a deep impression on them. During the last few weeks of her life, she was not with her little ones. Every morning, a friend came to fetch them, and they spent the day with her. One day, the children did not have time to say their prayers before starting. Celine, the Little Flower's sister, whispered to Little Therese. "Must we tell her that we have not said our prayers?" "Yes," answered Therese. So very timidly, Celine confided her secret to her. "Well, well, children, you shall say them." Then she took them to a large room, and left them there. They were astonished, and the Little Flower exclaimed: "This is not like Mamma. She always said our prayers with us." (p. 20)

After her beloved mother had passed on to her reward, the father took the mother's place in leading the children in prayer. Of this, St. Therese said:

"Later on, we went upstairs to pray, and there again I took my place next to my good father, and I had only to look at him to know how the saints pray." (p. 30) When Pauline tucked her into bed, Little Therese would ask her: "Have I been good today? Is the good God pleased with me? Do all the little angels want to fly around me?'" The answer was always, "Yes," otherwise she would have spent the whole night in tears.

When St. Therese was seven years old, she listened attentively as her sister, Celine, was instructed at home, in preparation for her First Holy Communion. At that time, children were not permitted to receive Our Blessed Lord in the Sacrament of His Love, until they were older. The Little Flower was eager to prepare herself, with Celine, and her heart swelled with grief when she was told that she was too young. One evening, she heard someone say to her happy little sister: "From the time of your First Communion, you must begin an entirely new life." At once, the Little Flower made a resolution not to wait until the time of her First Communion, but to begin with Celine. For "I thought four years was not too long to spend in making ready to receive Our dear Lord," said our Saint.

The Little Flower was not left to herself in choosing books for reading. She was not good at games, and so preferred to read. Her sisters were her visible guardian angels to guide her in this matter. She was allowed a limited time for this favorite recreation. As soon as the time had passed, it was her duty to stop instantly, even in the middle of a most interesting page. And she did so. In the course of her reading, the Little Flower read of the heroic deeds of past ages. Tales of chivalry thrilled her. It was at this time that Our Lord gave her a great grace. He made her understand that the only true glory is that which lasts forever; that to attain it, there is no need of brilliant deeds. She reflected that she was born for great things; that her personal glory would consist in becoming a Saint. Later, she was to say: "Believe me, the writing of pious books, the composing of the sublimest poetry, all that does not equal the smallest act of self-denial." (p. 271)

Many evenings as a child, the Little Flower spent much time in listening eagerly to her sister, Marie. Marie spoke of the imperishable riches which are so easy to amass each day, and of the folly of trampling them under foot, when one has but to stoop to gather them. How much good this did for our dear Saint is testified in her words: "It seems to me that all her great and generous heart passed over to me. As warriors of old trained their children in the skillful use of weapons, she trained me for the combat of life, arousing my ardor and showing me the glorious palm." (p. 56)

Celine and Therese were sisters in spirit as well as in the flesh. Many evenings, they went to the attic window, together, and looked out into the starry night. There, they talked of God and His divine love. Of this, St. Therese says: "The burning sparks that He scattered in our souls, the delicious, strong wine that He gave us to drink, caused all transitory things here below to disappear from our sight, and aspirations of love breathed forth from our lips." (p. 79)

God wills that we help one another in drawing ourselves to Him. This sweet responsibility which begins in the heart of the family, is shared by each of its members. And just as good is diffusive, the charity of the home must reach out to others. This responsibility touching the care of souls varies according to the office a person has in life. The greater is a person's responsibility in the care of souls, the more humble and little he should remain before God. The talents and gifts given him, are not for himself alone, but for the good of others, too. God chooses human instruments for the accomplishment of His work. Sometimes, a man laments because he is less gifted than another. He may believe that God loves him less, because less has been given him in intellectual and material gifts. On this matter, St. Therese says: "Ah! How true it is that God alone knows the depths of the heart! How limited are the

St. Therese Instructing the Carmelite Novices—E. Giaroli

"Lord, You see that I am too small to feed Your children,
(the Novices). If through me You wish to give each one
what it needs, fill my little hand ... and I will
distribute Your treasures. ..."

thoughts of creatures! When they see a soul whose lights surpass theirs, they conclude that God loves them less. But since when hasn't He had the right to use these creatures to dispense to His children the nourishment that is necessary to them? In the time of Pharaoh, even then He had this right, for in the Scriptures He says to the monarch: 'But this is why I have spared you: to show you My power and to make My name resound throughout the earth!'" (Exod. 9:16) (p. 179)

To help others to love God more, we must first love Him deeply ourselves. Through love we will lift ourselves and others to the embrace of Almighty God. Our good examples will bear fruit in proportion as divine love fills our heart. The Little Flower, at one time, was Novice Mistress in Carmel. As such, she was given great responsibility over souls. She considered herself too small spiritually to take care of their wants. So she prayed: "Lord, You see that I am too small to feed Your children. If through me You wish to give each one what it needs, fill my little hand; and without leaving Your arms, without even turning my head, I will distribute Your treasures to the soul that comes to me asking for her food. And so, knowing that it was impossible for me to do anything by myself, the task seemed simplified. I busied myself interiorly and solely in uniting myself more and more to God, knowing that the rest would be given to me over and above. In fact, my hope has never been deceived. My hand has always been found full every time it was necessary to nourish the soul of my Sisters. I assure you, Mother, if I ever acted otherwise, if I had relied on my own strength, I would have given up my weapons without delay." (p. 183)

Unfortunately, when some are given responsibility over souls, they do not remain little. They do not acknowledge that this task was given them by God. To them, Little Therese can say: "It is possible to remain little even in the most formidable assignments. For isn't it written that at the end of time: 'God arose for judgment, to save all the afflicted of the earth.' He does not say to judge, but to save." (Ps. 75:10) (p. 251)

Throughout her lifetime, the Little Flower gave example of many virtues. She strove to mirror the perfections of Jesus Christ. How well she did this, is seen by closely reading her Autobiography. Particularly noticeable is her love of God. Love prompted her to surrender herself completely to the infinite tenderness of God's embrace. The more perfectly she reflected God's love, the more perfectly she practised all the virtues. She was meek, patient, humble, obedient. She loved suffering as the road the Master had trod. And withal she was joyful, and at peace. How dear she must have been to the

Most Adorable Trinity. For in her pure life, she so closely resembled the Savior. She was worthy to call Mary her Mother.

Love was the key to all St. Therese's perfections. "How sweet is the way of love. Without doubt, one can fall, one can commit infidelities. But love, knowing how to draw profit from all things, has soon consumed all that displeases Jesus, leaving nothing in the depth of the heart, other than a humble, profound peace. Can I not sing with the psalmist that the 'Lord is good, for his kindness endures forever! (Ps. 107:1) It seems to me that if all creatures received the same favors, God would be feared by no one, but loved even to excess; and through love and not through fear, no soul would ever commit the least voluntary fault." (p. 146)

And, yet, all souls cannot be alike. They must differ from one another so that each Divine Perfection may receive special honor. To St. Therese, God gave His infinite mercy, and it was in that mirror that she contemplated all His other attributes. In that mirror, all His attributes appeared radiant with Love. Even His justice seemed clothed with love.

In the year 1895, St. Therese received the grace to understand more than ever how much Jesus desires to be loved. She thought of how many souls offered themselves as victims to the justice of God, in order to turn aside the punishment reserved for sinners, by taking them on themselves. Then it was that she cried out: "O my Divine Master, shall only Your justice receive victims of holocaust? Does not Your merciful love also have need of it? On all sides, it is misunderstood, rejected. Those hearts upon which You desire to lavish Your love, turn to creatures, searching for happiness in a miserable affection of the moment, instead of casting themselves in Your arms and accepting the delicious furnace of Your infinite love.

"O my God, must Your disdained love remain within Your heart? It seems to me that if You were to find souls offering themselves as victims of Your merciful love, You would consume them rapidly, that You would be happy to compress no longer the infinite tenderness that is locked up within You.

"If Your justice, which is had only upon earth, loves to release itself, how much more does not Your merciful love desire to embrace souls, since 'Your kindness reaches to heaven.' (Ps. 35:6) O Jesus, may I be that happy victim, consume Your little victim with the fire of Your love." (p. 147)

Immediately after she had made this oblation of herself to the merciful love of God, St. Therese tells us that she was "penetrated and surrounded with love." The wonderful effects of this surrendering of herself to the love of God, is testified to by our dear Saint's words: "Every moment, this merciful love renews me, purifies me and leaves in my heart no trace of sin. No. I no longer fear Purgatory. I know that I could not merit to enter even, with the Holy Souls in that place of expiation. But I also know that the fire of love is more sanctifying than that of Purgatory. I know that Jesus could not desire useless sufferings for us, and that He would not inspire me with desires that I feel, if He did not wish to fulfill them perfectly." (p. 148)

In these days, when the word "love" is so little understood and so often debased, may it not be that God, in His mercy, has given us St. Therese as an example to be imitated in true love? Can it not be that the words of the Holy Spirit may be applied to her: "But this is why I have spared you: to show you my power and to make my name resound throughout the earth!" (Ps. 9:16)

May God grant us the grace to imitate the Little Flower in the wonderful examples she has given us. And, like her, may we offer ourselves as little victims to the merciful love of God.

LOVE FOR THE
MOST BLESSED SACRAMENT

Such an ardent desire did Little Therese have to receive Jesus in Holy Communion, that she cried out: "Ah! I cannot receive Holy Communion as often as I desire. But Lord are You not All-Powerful? Remain in me as within a tabernacle. Never leave Your little victim.

"I would console You for the ingratitude of the wicked, and I beg You to take away my freedom to displease You. If through weakness I sometimes fall, may Your divine gaze immediately purify me, consuming all my imperfections just as fire transforms all things into itself." (p. 306)

This burning plea St. Therese made when she offered herself as a victim to the merciful love of God. Her heart was ever open to receive Jesus. In a letter written to her sister Celine, July 18, 1890, she says in part: "Dearest Celine, let us make a little tabernacle in our heart where Jesus can find refuge, then He will be consoled, and He will forget what we cannot forget—the ingratitude of souls who leave Him alone in a deserted tabernacle!

"Open to me, my sister, my beloved, my dove, my perfect one! For my head is wet with dew, my locks with the moisture of the night." (Cant. 5:2) That is what Jesus says to us when He is left alone and forgotten! . . . Celine, forgetfulness, I feel that is what causes Him most pain."

There is no devotion that will enkindle the heart with greater love of God than receiving Holy Communion. For in this Sacrament of Love, we become one with Jesus; there is perfect union with Jesus. For He Himself tells us: "He who eats My flesh, and drinks My blood, abides in Me and I in him." (John 6:57) If we receive Holy Communion every day, Jesus will always be with us and we will always advance in divine love.

But to prepare ourselves better for Holy Communion, we must be detached from creatures, and have a great desire to advance in divine love. By being detached from creatures is meant that the soul should be free of those affections that will lead us away from God. For the more of earthly love that is within the vessel of our soul, the less room there is for the love of God. In the second place, we must have a great desire to receive the living Body of Christ in Holy Communion. Jesus has a great desire to come into our souls; for that reason He remains night and day in the tabernacle, awaiting, calling and welcoming us. Should we not, then, also have a great desire to receive Jesus and His divine love, by Holy Communion?

St. Therese loved Jesus from the dawn of reason, and yearned for the day when she would receive Him sacramentally within her heart. She did not think four years too long to spend in making ready to receive our dear Lord. The Little Flower called her First Communion Day the "most beautiful day of all the days of my life." But she could not give us her inmost thoughts, for "one's inmost thoughts cannot be translated into earthly words without instantly losing their deep and heavenly meaning." But she does give us a glimpse into her beautiful soul, when she says: "Ah! How sweet was the first embrace of Jesus in my soul. Yes, it was an embrace of love! I felt myself loved, and I also said 'I love You and give myself to You forever!' Jesus asked nothing of me and claimed no sacrifice. For a long time already, He and Little Therese had known and understood each other. On that day, our meeting could not be called a simple recognition, but a union." (p. 59) She made her Communion on Ascension Day. Her tears flowed with inexpressible sweetness, and she kept repeating those words of St. Paul: "It is now no longer I that live, but Christ lives in me." (Gal. 2:20)

So ardently did St. Therese love Jesus, that she wished to find all her joy in Him. She wanted only the love of God to overwhelm her soul. And she prayed: "O Jesus, may I never seek or ever find but You alone! May creatures be nothing to me, and I, nothing to them! May nothing on earth disturb my peace." (p. 134)

It must not be thought that St. Therese did not have an affectionate heart. She herself tells us that once she loved, she always loved. But in all her affections, she drew herself closer to the Divine Lover, Jesus.

The Little Flower lived at a time when daily Communion was not practiced by the faithful. But she made it a practice to go to Holy Communion as often as her confessor allowed her. In later years, she acted quite differently. She tells us: "I am quite sure that a soul should tell her director the longing she has to receive her God. It isn't to dwell in the golden ciborium that He comes down from heaven each day, but so that He might find another heaven: the heaven of our soul, where He takes His delight." (p. 80)

While on a pilgrimage to Rome, the Little Flower visited the Holy House of Loreto. "At Loreto, this altar is found in the basilica, where the Holy House is enclosed like a precious diamond in a jewel-box of white marble. But this was not our concern. It was the diamond, the Bread of Angels, and not the jewel-box, that we wished to receive." (p. 101) St. Therese speaks of her ecstatic happiness in that Communion, saying: "The ineffable happiness of this holy communion! What then will it be when we communicate eternally in the dwelling of the King of Heaven? Then our joy will have no end, it will no longer be dimmed by the sadness of parting." (p. 101)

Everything associated with our dear Lord was most precious to St. Therese. When, as sacristan, she was permitted to handle the sacred vessels and the altar linens, her heart was deeply moved. She felt that she must increase in fervor, since she was so privileged to touch those sacred reminders of the Passion of Jesus.

All her life, the Little Flower was consumed with love for Jesus in the Most Blessed Sacrament. As a child, she loved to strew flowers before the Sacred Host. Whenever she went out for a walk with her dearly beloved father, she visited Jesus, the sweet Prisoner of Love in the tabernacle. The days seemed too far apart when she could approach the altar to take Jesus to her embrace. She was thoroughly conscious of the infinite tenderness and love Jesus had for her. Jesus filled her thoughts during her waking hours, and she marveled that since she thought of Him all day, she did not dream of Him at night!

On the vigil of the feast of Our Lady of Mt. Carmel, 1897, our dear Saint could not sleep, because of her great suffering. But while on her bed of pain, her thoughts sweetly turned to Jesus in the Sacrament of His Love, and she composed the following verses:

"You who know my utter insignificance
And do not hesitate to stoop to me!
O Sacrament I love, come to my heart;
Come to my heart, for it sighs for You.
On granting me this favor, Lord, I pray
That You would let me die of love.
O Jesus! Listen to love's plaintive cry
And come to my heart!

To die of love, the sweetest martyrdom this would be,
And such it is I desire to suffer so ardently.
O Cherubim! Your lyre now put in tune
For I feel my exile will end soon.
O Jesus Divine, fulfill my dream:
Let me die of love!"   (p. 242)

After St. Therese's second Communion, she felt irresistibly drawn towards suffering: "My heart became inflamed with a lively desire to suffer, and I felt an interior certainty that He had a great number of crosses in store for me. Then my soul was flooded with such consolations that I have never since experienced the like in my life. Suffering had a lure for me, and I found such charms in it, that it enraptured me, although as yet I did not understand it well." (p. 61)

What was it that so strongly attracted the Little Flower to the love of suffering? It was her desire to imitate Jesus in all things. The obedience, the docility, the patience of Jesus in the Most Blessed Sacrament filled her soul with longing to give Him the love others refused Him. But there are two sections of the Sacred Scripture that particularly pierced her heart with arrows of divine love. In the Book of Isaias (Ch. 53) she read:

"Who would believe what we have heard? To whom has the arm of the Lord been revealed? He grew up like a sapling before him, like a shoot from the parched earth; there was in him no stately bearing to make us look at him, nor appearance that would attract us to him. He was spurned and avoided by men, a man of suffering, accustomed to infirmity, one of those from whom men hide their faces, spurned, and we held him in no esteem. Yet it was our infirmities that he bore, our sufferings that he endured, while we thought of him as stricken, as one smitten by God and afflicted. But he was pierced for our offences, crushed for our sins; upon him was the chastisement that makes us whole, by his stripes we were healed." (Isaias: 53:1-5)

"Who is this that comes from Edom, in crimsoned garments, from Bosra—this one arrayed in majesty, marching in the greatness of his strength? 'It is I, I who announce vindication, I who am mighty to save. 'Why is your apparel red, and your garments like those of the wine presser? 'The wine press I have trodden alone, and of my people there was no one with me. I trod them in my anger, and trampled them down in my wrath; their blood spurted on my garments; all my apparel I stained. For the day of vengeance was in my heart, my year for redeeming was at hand. I looked about, but there was no one to lend support." (Isaias 63:1-5)

St. Therese wrote a letter to her sister, Celine, July 18, 1890, in which she also enclosed the above passages. Of them, she says: "I am sending you a passage from Isaias that will console you. See what a long time ago it was! And yet the soul of the prophet, like ours, was immersed in the hidden beauties of the Holy Face.... That was centuries ago! Ah! I ask myself, what is time? Time is but a mirage, a dream. God already sees us in glory. He enjoys our eternal beatitude. How much good this thought does to my soul! Then I understand why He permits us to suffer.... Very well, since our Beloved has 'trodden the wine press alone' He gives us to drink. On our part, we must not refuse to wear vestments stained with blood, and to tread for Jesus a new wine that will quench His thirst. Then looking about, He will no longer see that He is alone, for we will be there to give Him aid." (p. 324)

It seems that in writing the history of her soul, our beloved Saint was captivated by two words: "love" and "suffering." Love, divine love, was her soul's most ardent desire. Her means of expressing her love was through the imitation of Christ in His suffering. The practice of all other virtues sprang from the love she bore Jesus. Contemplating Jesus, hidden in the Most Blessed Sacrament, her soul burned with desire to love Him and to prove her love even in her most trifling actions.

The devout Thomas á Kempis tells us that "many run to sundry places to visit the relics of the Saints, and wonder to hear of their remarkable deeds; they behold the spacious buildings of their churches, and kiss their sacred bones, enveloped in silk and gold:

"And behold Thou art here present to me on the altar, my God, the Saint of Saints, the Creator of Men, and the Lord of Angels.

"Oftentimes in seeing those things men are moved with curiosity and the novelty of sights, and carry home but little fruit of amendment; and the more so when persons run lightly hither and thither without real contrition.

"But here, in the Sacrament of the altar, Thou art wholly present, my God, the man Christ Jesus; where also is derived, in full copiousness, the fruit of eternal salvation, as often as Thou art worthily and devoutly received.

"To this, indeed, we are not drawn by any levity, curiosity, or sensuality, but by a firm faith, a devout hope, and a sincere charity." (Imitation, Book IV, Ch. 1)

Our beloved Little Sister, the strong, fragrant Flower of God, always came to the heart of things. Her entire life revolved about the Eucharistic Heart of Jesus and the Most Adorable Trinity. Just as a flower reaches out its sweet blooms in whatever direction the sun may be, so, too, did the Little Flower of Jesus strain towards God in whatever occupation she found herself. Truly, she was a saint of ardent desires!

She was privileged to visit many shrines of the Saints and to venerate the sacred relics of God's loved ones. And in all this, her heart expanded with greater love for Jesus. All that she thought of, all that she desired, all that she hoped for, all that she

St. Therese in Prayer—E. Giaroli

"Behold Thou art here present to me on the altar, my God,
the Saint of Saints, the Creator of Men, and the Lord of Angels."

had, all that she loved, were as so many threads that bound her ever more intimately and closely to the Infinite God of Love.

Oh! how we ought to imitate St. Therese in her ardent desires to receive Jesus into our hearts in Holy Communion. With what eagerness should we approach the altar to receive the Bread of Angels! For in this Blessed Sacrament, we receive God in all His perfections. We receive the fullness of the Divinity of Jesus, all the virtues and graces of His humanity, and all the merits of the Man-God! Jesus can do no more for us, for in giving us Himself, He has given us All.

In the Most Blessed Sacrament, Jesus has left us a memorial of His Passion. How sad it is that so many forget Him in this Sacrament of His Love. "Forgetfulness, I feel that that is what causes Him most pain," says St. Therese. Oh, let us never forget Jesus, so lovingly awaiting us. Let us take Him to our hearts in fondest and sweetest embrace and say: O my Jesus, I love You. Give me Your love and Your grace and the strength always to do Your Will. I ask for nothing more.

LOVE FOR OUR BLESSED MOTHER

The last words written by St. Therese were: "O Mary, were I Queen of Heaven, and were you Therese, I should wish to be Therese that I might see you Queen of Heaven!" This delicate, spontaneous uplifting of her heart to the sweet Mother of God was the cry of love that had grown with her from her childhood. Because of the divine love that filled her soul, she was able to say with St. John of the Cross: "All is mine, all is for me; the earth is mine, the heavens are mine, God is mine, and the Mother of God is mine."

On the nineteenth of October, 1892, our Saint wrote a letter to her dearest Celine, and she has this to say: "Incidentally, concerning the Blessed Virgin, I must confide to you one of my simplicities. Sometimes, I surprise myself in saying to her: 'Do you know, dear Mother, that I am more fortunate than you? I have you for a Mother, and like me, you do not have a Blessed Virgin to love! It is true that you are the Mother of Jesus, but you have given Him to me. And He, on the Cross, gave you to us as our Mother. And so we are richer than you are! In times gone by, in your humility you sighed to become the little servant of the Mother of God. And I, poor little creature, I am not your servant, but your child! You are the Mother of Jesus and you are my Mother." (p. 330)

Thoughts of Jesus and Mary were woven in St. Therese's soul, as so many red roses and white lilies. Towards the closing days of her life, she revealed some of her inmost thoughts, forced, as it were, by the pressure of love. One evening, she exclaimed: "How I love the Virgin Mary! If I had been a priest, how eloquently I would have spoken about her! She is shown as unapproachable. She should be shown as imitable. She is more mother than queen! I have heard it said that her brilliance eclipses all the saints, just as the sun on rising causes the stars to disappear. My God! But that is strange! A mother who makes disappear the glory of her children! For my part, I think just the opposite. I believe that she will increase still more the splendor of the elect. . . . The Virgin Mary! How simple, it seems to me, her life must have been!" (p. 241)

Having come from a devout, Catholic family, little Therese was taught the heavenly truths from babyhood. Love for the Mother of Jesus was deeply rooted in her soul. On the occasion of her first Confession the priest exhorted her to a tender devotion to Our Lady. "And," St. Therese adds, "I promised myself to redouble my love for her, who already held a very large place in my heart." (p. 27) Our beloved Saint told her prayers to the Mother of God, using those prayers taught her by her dear parents. She was encouraged in her devotions; and during the beautiful month of May, erected a little altar at home, where she devoutly honored Our Blessed Mother. Nor was her love for the Queen of Heaven to go unrewarded, even in this life. Gifts, both spiritual and temporal, were granted her in abundance.

God was pleased to try His chosen little one by grave sickness. For a time, she hovered between life and death. A ten-year-old child, she bore her suffering with heroic patience. When her sufferings grew less, she found great delight in weaving garlands of daisies and forget-me-nots for Our Lady's statue. "We were then in the beautiful month of May, and all nature was clothed with springtime flowers. Only the little flower drooped and seemed to have withered forever! However, she had a sun above her, and this sun was the Queen of Heaven. Often, very often, the little flower turned her crown towards this blessed Star." (p. 47) When the illness gradually became worse, her father had a novena of Masses offered in Paris, at Our Lady of Victories shrine. During the novena, Little Therese became extremely sick. She was in unutterable anguish. Marie, Leonie and Celine tried to comfort her, without avail. She seemed at the point of death. In their great sorrow, they turned tearful eyes to Our Lady, and begged her help. Little Therese, finding no help on earth and nearly dead with pain, turned to her Heavenly Mother, begging from the bottom of her heart, that she have pity on her. "All at once, the statue came to life! The Virgin Mary became beautiful, so beautiful that I have never found words to express this heavenly beauty. Her face expressed sweetness, goodness, ineffable love. But what pierced me to the very depth of my soul, was her ravishing smile! Then all my suffering vanished and two big tears gushed to my eyes and fell silently!" (p. 49)

Mary, Mother of God, was drawn in tender mercy, not only to comfort the Little Flower's father and her sisters, but to show special love for this child dear to her heart. And well did Little Therese understand the love of Mary. As ever, she returned love for love. Speaking of her debt to Mary, St. Therese, on the occasion of her First Holy Communion said: "It seems to me that she looked upon her little flower with love and smiled on her again. I remember her visible smile that had at another time healed and delivered me. I knew well what

I owed her! Had not she herself come to me the
morning of May 8th and placed in the chalice of
my soul 'a flower of Saron, a lily of the valley' "
(Cant. 2:1) (p. 60)

St. Therese knew that all graces come to us
through Mary, for God so wills it. Thinking on
Mary, she pictured her grace-giving role in many
attractive ways. On her First Holy Communion Day,
she imagined her soul like a garden. Mary was the
heavenly gardener, who planted the sweetest of
Flowers, Jesus, in this holy soil. When she entered
Carmel, St. Therese pictured herself as a little white
flower, being transplanted by Mary from the good
earth of her family circle, to the more fertile and life-
giving earth of the cloister. At other times, Our
Blessed Mother is portrayed as she really is, a Mother. "At the moment of Communion, I sometimes
picture my soul as a baby three or four years old,
that, through its activity at play, has its hair dishev-
elled and clothing soiled. These misfortunes have
befallen me in struggling with souls. But soon the
Virgin Mary hurries about me. She quickly makes
me take off my pinafore, all soiled, sets my hair, and
adorns it with a pretty ribbon or simply a tiny flower. And that is enough to make me graceful, and to
sit without blushing at the Banquet of the Angels."
(p. 295) At other times, our sweet Lady is pictured as a grand architect. Little Therese pictured

her soul as a waste ground, and begged our Blessed Mother to take away all her imperfections—which she called 'heaps of rubbish'—and to build upon it a splendid tabernacle worthy of Heaven, and adorn it with her *own* adornments! At times, our gracious Lady is portrayed as a wonder-worker, who changes bitter things into sweet, sorrows into joys. In her letter of February 24, 1896, she says to her sister: "For love, Celine will henceforth press to her heart the thorns of suffering and contempt, but she is not afraid, knowing of her own experience that Mary can change into milk the blood that pours from the wounds made by love. With her left hand, Celine grasps the thorns, but with her right, she continues to keep hold on Jesus, the divine bundle of myrrh resting upon her heart."

The love of Our Blessed Mother for souls is like that of the Divine Physician. She heals wounds, strengthens and comforts, and finally brings the soul to perfect rest. For all those who give themselves as martyrs to the divine Love, St. Therese addresses the words she sent to a missionary, in her letter of May 9, 1897: "How can He purify in the flames of Purgatory souls consumed in the fires of divine love? Of course no human life is free from faults, only the Immaculate Virgin presents herself in absolute purity before God's Majesty. What a joy to remember that she is our Mother! Since she loves

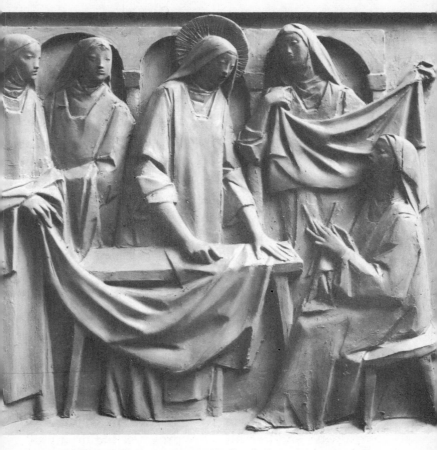

St. Therese Doing Community Duties—E. Giaroli

"I found the religious life what I thought it should be.
No sacrifice surprises me. And yet you know
that in my first steps I came across more
thorns than roses."

us and knows our weakness, what have we to fear? What a lot of phrases to express my thought, or rather, to manage not to express it; I simply wanted to say that it seems to me that all missionaries are martyrs by desire and will, and that, in consequence, not one should go to Purgatory. If, at the moment they appear before God, some traces of human weakness remain in their souls, the Blessed Virgin obtains for them the grace to make an act of perfect love, and then gives them the palm and the crown they have truly merited."

Mary is pictured as a Giver of Gifts. When the Little Flower was on her pilgrimage to Rome, she prayed at the shrine of Our Lady of Victories, in Paris. "What I experienced in her shrine," says St. Therese, "I could never tell you. The graces she bestowed on me seemed like those of my First Holy Communion. I was filled with peace and happiness. It was there that my Mother, the Virgin Mary, told me clearly that it was she who had smiled and cured me. With what fervor I begged her to watch over me always and to realize my dream of hiding myself under the shade of her virginal mantle! I also asked her again to keep me far from all the occasions of sin." (p. 95)

On the feast of the Nativity of Mary, the Little Flower became the spouse of Jesus, by the vows of her holy profession. How does our dear Saint picture herself? She imagines the little new-born Holy Virgin as a baby, clutching a little flower in her hand, to present to the Little Jesus. She herself is the flower, so lovingly held within the fingers of the Virgin. And speaking of Mary's goodness to her, the Little Flower says: "That day everything was little except the graces I received—except the peace and joy in gazing upon the beautiful star-lit sky at night, and in thinking that soon I should fly away to Heaven and be united to my Divine Spouse amid eternal bliss."

There is a little prayer, which St. Therese tells us, includes all her desires. She was anxious that it be said for her. And this is the prayer: "Merciful Father, in the name of our sweet Jesus, of the Virgin Mary and the saints, I ask you to inflame my sister with Your spirit of Love and grant her the grace to make You greatly loved." It was through Mary that Little Therese delighted to come to Jesus, the Beloved of her soul. It is good to note that this brief prayer was written on February 24, 1897, and that St. Therese had offered herself as a burnt-offering to the merciful love of God on June 9, 1895. In brief words, our Saint sums up all her heart's desires. In giving herself utterly and completely to the Adorable Trinity, she willed to do so through the Mother of God. This we know from her words: "Finally, I offer You, O Blessed Trinity, the love and the merits of the Blessed Virgin Mary, my dear Mother. To her, I abandon my offering and beg her to present it to You." (p. 305)

On February 23, 1896, St. Therese sweetly composed a "Contract of Marriage between Jesus and Celine." There are many inspiring sentiments in this delightful contract, one of which is: "I, the Flower of the fields, the Lily of the valleys, will give my beloved for her nourishment the Wheat of the Elect, the 'wine that springs forth virgins,' . . . She will receive this food from the hands of the humble and glorious Virgin Mary, the Mother of us both."

During her precious lifetime, St. Therese sought and obtained all good things from the Mother of God. Jesus was well pleased with her in this, and filled her soul to the brim and overflowing with love and tender care. For this reason she was able to cry out: "All my desires have been satisfied, not only my desires for perfection, but even those whose vanity I understood without having experienced them." (p. 141) And again: "Yes, I repeat, He has always given me what I desired, or rather, He has made me desire what He wished to give me." (p. 196) And our dear Saint goes on to say: "Ah! How happy the Lord makes me! How sweet and easy it is to serve Him on earth!" (p. 196) Because St. Therese understood Mary's part in our Redemption, she invoked Our Blessed Mother often, both in times of joy and in times of trial.

While she was in her terrible death-agony, that lasted twelve hours, she called out: "O my God! O sweet Virgin Mary! come to my aid." She did come to her aid, and gave her those graces that made her die a victim of the merciful love of the good God.

May we, in imitation of our beloved St. Therese, remain in the loving embrace of Mary, Our Mother. Through her maternal care, we will joyfully be led to the closest union with her Divine Son, Jesus.

PART II

Meditations

on the

Litany of the

Little Flower

LITANY OF THE LITTLE FLOWER

Lord have mercy on us.
Christ have mercy on us.
Lord have mercy on us.
Christ hear us.
God the Father of Heaven,
God the Son, Redeemer of the world,

Have mercy on us.

God the Holy Spirit,
Holy Trinity, One God,
Holy Mary,
Holy Mother of God,
Holy Virgin of Virgins,

Pray for us.

Our Lady of Mt. Carmel,
Our Lady of Victory,
Saint Therese of the Child Jesus,
Saint Therese of the Holy Face,
Little Flower of Jesus,
Youthful Spouse of the Holy Spirit,
Special Favorite of Mary,
Favored by Her Heavenly Smile,
Devoted Child of St. Joseph,
Beloved daughter of Saint Teresa,

Pray for us.

Faithful Follower of St. John of the Cross,
Child of predilection from thy infancy,
Angel of the Cloister,
Seraph of the Altar,
Most perfect Religious,
Abandoned to the Will of God,
Fortress of Trust and Confidence,
Teaching God's Mercy,
Poor in desires,
Chaste Dove,
Beautiful Flower of Carmel,
Fragrant Lily of Purity,
Sweet Rose of charity,
Modest Violet of humility, -
Shedding sweet perfumes upon the earth,
Patroness of Missionaries,
Zealous Guardian of the Clergy,
Converter of hardened hearts,
Kind Physician of the maladies of the soul,
Worker of prodigies,
Wonder of our age,
Vessel of God's Power,
Helper in our many needs.

Saint Therese who did love God so ardently,
Who had such wonderful trust in Him,
Who while immersed in the love of God wert yet a
"little victim,"
Who said you would "let fall a shower of roses"
after your death,
Who said you would "spend your Heaven in doing good
upon earth,"
Who said you "would not take your rest until the
last soul was garnered in,"
Who told us to call you "Little Therese,"

Pray for us.

Pray for us.

Obtain our petitions

Who breathed forth your pure soul in an Act of the Love of God,
Lamb of God, etc.
Pray for us Saint Therese of the Child Jesus,
That we may follow in your "little way" and that our last words
may be like yours: "My God, I love Thee!"

LET US PRAY

Merciful Father, in the words of St. Therese, I beg of
Thee in the Name of Thy sweet Jesus, of the Blessed Virgin
and of the Saints, to inflame me with Thy spirit of love and
to grant me the grace of winning much love for Thee. Amen.

NIHIL OBSTAT:

Sti. Ludovici, die 12 Apr. 1927.
Joannes Rothensteiner,
Censor Librorum.

IMPRIMATUR:

Sti. Ludovici, die 13 Apr. 1927.
Joannes J. Glennon,
Archiep. Sti. Ludovici.

ST. THERESE OF THE CHILD JESUS

Our dear Saint wondered one day what name would be given to her later on, when she entered the convent. She knew that there was already a Sister of Teresa of Jesus, at Carmel. Nevertheless, her beautiful name Therese could not be taken from her. She tells us: "Suddenly, I thought of the Child Jesus whom I loved so much, and I said to myself: 'Oh! How happy I would be to be called Therese of the Child Jesus!' However, I was very careful not to express my desire. And behold, Mother Prioress said to me in the midst of her conversation: 'When you come amongst us, my dear little girl, you will be called Therese of the Infant Jesus!' My joy was great. And this happy meeting of our thoughts seemed to me a gentle kindness from my beloved little Jesus!" (p. 53)

How tenderly Little Therese loved the Infant Jesus is testified to in her written word. In a letter dated February, 1884, she says in part: "You don't know what happiness I felt when Marie showed me your lovely little book. I found it entrancing; I had never seen anything so beautiful, and I could not take my eyes off it. What lovely prayers at the beginning! I said them to the little Child Jesus with all my heart. Every day I try to do all the 'practices' I can, and I do my best not to let any opportunity pass. From the bottom of my heart and as often as possible I say the little prayers: they are sweet-scented roses. What a beautiful picture in the front! It is a little dove giving its heart to the Child Jesus. That's what I'll do with mine! I intend to adorn it with all the lovely flowers I find, so as to offer it to the Child Jesus on the day of my First Holy Communion; and truly, as it says in the little prayer at the beginning of the book, I want the Child Jesus to be so happy in my heart that He won't think of going back to heaven. . . ."

While on a pilgrimage to Rome, she visited the Holy House of Loreto. Of this, our sweet Saint says: "I found Loreto enchanting. But what shall I say of the Holy House? My emotions were very profound on finding myself under the same roof that had sheltered the Holy Family, on contemplating the walls on which our Savior had fixed His divine eyes, in walking on the ground that St. Joseph had moistened with his sweat, where Mary had carried Jesus in her arms, after having borne Him in her virginal womb. I saw the little room of the Annunciation. I placed my rosary in the little bowl of the Infant Jesus. How sweet are these memories!" (p. 100)

St. Therese had offered herself to be His little plaything. "I told Him not to treat me like one of those expensive toys that children are content to look at, but dare not touch, but like a little ball of no value that He could throw on the ground, kick about, pierce, leave in a corner, or even press to His heart, if that gave Him pleasure. In a word, I wanted to amuse the Infant Jesus and to abandon myself to His childish whims. He was to hear my prayer! At Rome, Jesus pierced His little toy. Without doubt, He wanted to see what it had inside. And then satisfied with His discovery, He let His little ball fall, and fell asleep. What did He do during His sweet slumber? Jesus dreamed that He was still playing with it, that He took it and left it in turn, that He made it roll far away. But finally He pressed it to His heart, never more permitting it to leave His little hand. You can imagine the sadness of the little ball on finding itself on the ground! And yet it continued to hope against hope." (p. 7)

Our beloved Saint was conscious that God showered many graces on her. She had a constant desire to advance in virtue, but often her actions were spoiled by imperfections. She was extremely sensitive. But the time had come when Our Lord wished to free her from childhood's failings, and even withdraw from her its innocent pleasures. It was Christmas Day, 1886. Then it was that the Child Jesus strengthened her. Says our dear Saint, "On the feast of Christmas, on that blessed night, Jesus, sweet Infant of an hour, changed the darkness of my soul into torrents of light. In becoming weak and small for love of me, He made me strong and brave. He armed me with His weapons, and then I marched on from victory to victory, beginning, so to speak, 'to walk like a giant.' (Ps. 18:5) My fountain of tears was dried up, and opened only with difficulty and rarely." (p. 74)

When St. Therese entered Carmel, she wished for snow. And she tells us: "Have I told you, Mother, how fond I am of snow? When I was a little girl, its whiteness entranced me. Where did this love for snow come from? Perhaps, since I was a little winter flower, the first garment which my infant eyes saw clothing the earth was this white cloak. I then wished to see nature dressed in white, like me, on the day when I would take my Habit. But that evening, the temperature was so mild, that one could almost believe it was Spring, and I no longer hoped for snow. At ten o'clock in the morning, there was no change! I then gave up my childish desire as impossible to be realized." (p. 123) After the ceremony in the Chapel, when she had once more set foot in the enclosure, her eyes fell on the statue of the Child Jesus, smiling on her amid the flowers and lights. Then, turning towards the quadrangle, she saw, that in spite of the mildness of the weather, it was covered with snow! Of this, she says: "What a delicate attention on the part of Jesus. Fulfilling the desires of His betrothed, He gave her snow! Who is that mortal, powerful as he may be, who can make fall from the sky just one snowflake to please his beloved?" (p. 125)

PRAYER

My dearly beloved St. Therese, so inflamed with love towards the Child Jesus that you wished Him to be so happy within your heart that He would not think of going back to Heaven, pray for me, that those same dispositions may fill my soul. Just as every child should have a plaything, you gave yourself to be the Divine Infant's toy; and you did so, so completely, that He pressed you to His Heart, never to let you go! Oh, may I offer myself in like manner to this Adorable Child, that He will take full possession of me and keep me as a treasured toy, to delight His Sacred Heart.

Dearest Infant Jesus, I dare to take You into my arms, to caress You, to adore You, to kiss Your Sacred lips. O Divine Child, consume me with Your Love. I give myself to You without reserve, and beg You to accomplish Your Divine Will in me. Amen.

ST. THERESE OF THE HOLY FACE

The soul of St. Therese was deeply affected when she read the words of the Prophet Isaias, concerning Jesus.

She tells us: "Up until then, I had not sounded the depths of the treasures locked up in the Holy Face. It was my dear Mother, Agnes of Jesus, who taught me to know them. Just as she had preceded her three sisters into Carmel, even so she was the first to penetrate the mysteries of love hidden in the Face of our Spouse. Then she unveiled them to me, and I understood. I understood better than ever, what true glory is. He whose kingdom is not of this world, showed me that the only enviable royalty consists in wanting to be ignored and counted for nothing, to put her joy in contempt of self. Ah! How I wished that like the Face of Jesus, my face would be hidden from the eyes of all, that no one on earth would know me. I thirsted to suffer and to be forgotten." (p. 121)

Often and delicately does St. Therese speak of the Holy Face, and her meditations caused a holy fire to spring within her heart. In a letter to her sister, Celine, of August, 1893, she says: "My dear Celine, let us rejoice in our lot. Let us give and give to our Beloved. Let us be prodigal towards Him, but let us never forget that He is a Hidden Treasure: few souls know how to discover it. To find a hidden thing, it is necessary to hide oneself, that our life be one of mystery. 'Do you want to learn something that may serve you?' says the Imitation: 'love to be ignored and accounted for nothing. . . .' And in another place: 'After you have left everything, you must above all leave yourself; let one man boast of one thing, one of another; for you, place your joy only in contempt of yourself.' " (p. 333)

Throughout her life, our dearly beloved Saint sought to be humble and very small. She oftentimes called herself a "little grain of sand" that is light, that can be easily overlooked and easily carried. She desired nothing more than to be forgotten. She did not want contempt, nor insults, for such things would be too much glory for a "grain of sand." To be despised it would have to be seen, but she wanted to be *forgotten!* Not only did she want to be forgotten by creatures, but also by herself. She desired to be so reduced to nothing, as to have no desire left. All she sought was the glory of Jesus. She abandoned her own to Him.

Thus did she pray to the Holy Face:

"O Adorable Face of Jesus, sole beauty which ravishes my heart, deign to impress upon my soul Your Divine Likeness, so that You cannot look upon the soul of Your little spouse without contemplating Yourself. O my Beloved, for love of You I accept not being able to see the sweetness of Your glance, not to feel the inexpressible kiss of Your mouth, but I beg You to encompass me with Your love so that it will consume me quickly, and soon cause me to appear before You: Therese of the Holy Face." (p. 310)

PRAYER

My dearest Sister, St. Therese, your heart was so delicately attuned to the inspirations of the Holy Spirit, that when you thought on the Holy Face of Jesus, you efficaciously desired to be hidden and despised even as He. Since you are my beloved Sister, given to me by God as a heavenly guide, obtain for me the grace to imitate you in the depths of your humility and self-abasement. May my sole desire be that of giving pleasure to Jesus, in this life and for all eternity. Amen.

LITTLE FLOWER OF JESUS

St. Therese of the Child Jesus, was born on January 2, 1873. In the course of the day, a poor child rang timidly at the door of the happy home, and presented a simple stanza:

"Smile and swiftly grow,
All invites you to happiness,
Tender love; tender care . . .
Yes, smile at the dawn,
Bud about to bloom,
One day you will be a rose!" (p. 17)

In later years, this beloved child looked at the book of nature. And in the gladness of her heart, she considered the world of souls, Our Lord's living garden. She knew that if a little flower could speak, it would tell quite simply all that God had done for it, without hiding any of its gifts. It would not, under the pretext of humility, say that it had not a sweet scent, that the sun had withered its petals, or the storm bruised its stem, if it knew that such were not the case. Little Therese then called herself

"The Little Flower." And she went on to say: "She knows that there was nothing in her capable of attracting His divine glance, and that only His mercy has filled her to overflowing with good things. It is He who caused her to grow in holy ground enriched with the perfume of purity. It is He who had her preceded by eight lilies of shining whiteness. In His love, He wished her to be preserved from the poisoned breath of the world. Hardly had her petals begun to unfold, when the good Master transplanted her to Carmel, in the chosen garden of the Virgin Mary." (p. 7)

In those few words, she summed up all that God's goodness had done for her.

Our dear Saint loved to compare souls to flowers, and did so often. In a letter written to her dearest Celine, in April, 1891, she says in part: "He created a small unnoticed flower called Celine. He wants His little flower to save Him souls, and for that He wants only one thing, that His flower should look at Him while it suffers its martyrdom . . . and this mysterious gaze passing between Jesus and His small flower will work marvels and will give Jesus a multitude of other flowers, particularly a certain faded, withered lily that must be changed into a rose of love and repentance."

In July of 1888, St. Therese had written to Celine: "I used to sometimes wonder why Jesus took me first. Now I understand. You see, your soul is a Lily-Immortelle. Jesus can do whatever He will with it. It makes little difference whether it is in this place or that. Always it will be an Immortelle. The wind cannot scatter the yellow of the Lily's stamens over its fragrant white calyx. Jesus made it so. He is free and none can ask Him why He gives His graces to one soul rather than another. Alongside this lily, Jesus placed another, its faithful companion. They grew up together, but one was Immortelle, the other was not; and Jesus had to take His lily before the blossom began to open, that both lilies might be for Him. . . . One was frail, the other strong. Jesus took the weak and left the other to grow to a lovelier flowering. . . . Jesus demands *all* of His two lilies, He wills that they keep nothing but their white garment. . . . *All.* Has the Immortelle understood its little sister?"

Once, when a good Sister of the community wished to go without Holy Communion because of an imperfection of which she had repented, St. Therese sent her this touching note: "Little flower, Jesus' dear one, it suffices well enough that for your humiliation of soul, your roots eat the earth. . . . It is necessary that you open your petals, or rather, lift up your head, so that the Bread of Angels comes, like the divine dew, to strengthen you and give you all that you are lacking. Good night, poor little flow-

er, ask that all the prayers which are said for my
cure be used to increase the fire that must consume
me." (p. 294)

Using the words of the angelic martyr, Theo-
phane Venard, our beloved St. Therese wrote: "I
am a spring flower which the Divine Master culls
for His pleasure. We are all flowers, planted on this
earth, and God will gather us in His own good time
—some sooner, some later. . . . I, little flower of one
day, am the first to be gathered! But we shall meet
again in Paradise, where lasting joy will be our
portion."

How beautiful is Little Therese's poem entitled
"To Scatter Flowers."

"Jesus, my only love, at the foot of your Calvary,
How I would love each evening to scatter flowers!
In shedding the petals of the springtime flower,
I would dry Your tears!

To scatter flowers . . . that is to offer You the first-fruits,
The lightest sighs, the greatest sorrows.
My sufferings, my little sacrifices:
Behold my flowers!

Lord, my soul is captivated by Your beauty;
I would lavish my perfume and my flowers upon You.
On scattering them on the wing of a breeze
I would inflame hearts!

To scatter flowers! Jesus, behold the weapons
With which I would wrestle to save sinners.
The victory is mine: I always disarm You
With my flowers!

The petals of the flowers caress Your Face
They tell You that my heart is Yours without return.

From my rose unpetalled, ah! You know the language,
And You smile at my love. . . .

To scatter flowers! To return Your praises,
Behold my pleasure on the shore of tears.
Soon I will come to heaven with the little angels,
To scatter flowers!" (p. 403)

PRAYER

Dearest St. Therese, chosen Little Flower of Jesus, pray that I blossom into that beauty that God has destined for me, so that I may gladden His divine eyes and bring joy to His Sacred Heart. Plead for me, that Jesus heal this bruised and withered flower, that I may have that flush of loveliness He desires. Amen.

YOUTHFUL SPOUSE OF THE HOLY SPIRIT

What is a spouse, but a partner in marriage? In this sacred relationship, bride and groom give one another to each other. They are one in thought, one in mind and one in affection. This union is a type of the union which exists between Christ and His Church. It is also a type of the union that exists between a soul in the state of grace and the Holy Spirit. For every soul possessing sanctifying grace is truly a spouse of the Holy Spirit.

When a young maiden enters the convent or the cloister, she is often referred to as a Spouse of Christ, for now she must, in a particular way, be one in mind, one in thought and one in affections with Christ Jesus. St. Therese of the Child Jesus was the dearly beloved daughter of the Father, the sweet bride of Christ and the youthful spouse of the Holy Spirit. For the Adorable Trinity took full possession of her, so much so that her entire life was spent in God, for God and with God. She abandoned herself utterly to the inspirations of the Holy Spirit.

The Holy Spirit is referred to as the Spirit of Love. Little Therese was held captive by Love, surrendered herself to Love, lived and died in Love. From the dawn of reason, she denied the good God nothing. Under the promptings of the Holy Spirit, she gave herself completely to God. She retained her baptismal innocence all through life. Truly, then, was she the "Youthful Spouse of the Holy Spirit."

In all the important affairs of her life, our beloved Saint had recourse to the Holy Spirit. When she had resolved to enter Carmel, she sought means to tell her saintly father. It was but natural that she should turn to the Divine Comforter, for long had she been most intimate with Him. She goes on to tell us: "I chose the feast of Pentecost to make my great disclosure. All that day, I asked for light from the Holy Spirit, begging the Apostles to pray for me and to inspire me with the words I should use. In fact, were they not the ones who ought to come to the help of a timid child whom God had destined to become the apostle of apostles through prayer and sacrifice." (p. 83)

St. Therese had a deep insight into spiritual truths. Her love and understanding of the Sacred Scriptures, which are the Words of the Holy Spirit, reveal the depth of her love of God. God's Words were engraven on her heart and lived in action in her soul. The beauty of the Little Flower's soul in union with the Holy Spirit can be seen, even though greatly veiled, in the written words she has left us in her Autobiography and in her letters. She so loved the Holy Bible that she always carried it close to her heart.

The word "love" appears on almost every page of the ascetical works of the great Redemptorist and Doctor of Prayer, St. Alphonsus Mary de Liguori, for the Holy Spirit had enkindled Its burning flame within his soul. In much the same way, St. Therese used the word "love." It is found hundreds of times in her letters and her Autobiography. To ennumerate them all would well nigh fill a book. And all her expressions are like burning torches, revealing the depth of divine love that the Holy Spirit had enkindled within her.

St. Pius X, after he had read the Autobiography, wrote: "This book, wherein shines forth the virtues of Soeur Therese of Lisieux, and into which it may be said that her whole soul has passed, has been to Us a source of most sweet joy. Verily, she blossomed as a lily, and she has shed abroad the lily's pleasing perfume. She has put forth a rich fruitage of Divine Grace, and praised to the full her Lord, and blessed Him in His works." (From the Vatican, Nov. 7, 1910)

On Easter, 1910, Desiré Cardinal Mercier, Archbishop of Malines' wrote in part concerning our dear St. Therese: "The soul whose tender beauty you unveil to your readers is like the hyacinth and the other springtide blossoms whose fragrance makes us forget the frosts of winter; and by the shafts of light wherein they are bathed we rise to the resplendent sun that, in a little while, will turn the harvest to gold. No one can read a life such as that of Sister Therese of the Child Jesus without the soul expanding, without a feeling of peace, and without experiencing more keenly the attractions of Divine Love.

"Where can we better follow the divinely triumphant action of the Spirit of God? We see how this innocent child fears to wound God's Fatherly Heart, how she dedicates herself so completely to His service, and becomes a victim for the Church and for souls. We note the unerring judgment that discerns the true from the false, the good from the bad; the strength of will that leads a girl of fifteen to heroic virtue. Truly, the Counsellor from on High guided each step of this lofty soul—all steeped in grace—whose every thought was illumined by our holy Faith. Always and everywhere true wisdom kept her in union with God, and love for God was her source of inspiration.

"Wisdom, understanding, counsel, fortitude, knowledge, piety, fear of the Lord—these gifts

St. Therese in Prayer—E. Giaroli

"At last I have found my vocation! My vocation is love! Yes, I have found my vocation in the bosom of the Church, and it is You, O my God, Who have given me this place."

abound in the heart of Therese, and through their human tabernacle, translucent as crystal, these marvellous graces shine forth.

PRAYER

Dearest St. Therese, pray for me that like you, I may be one in thought, one in mind and one in affections with the inspirations of the Holy Spirit. From this day forth, may I deny the good God nothing.

SPECIAL FAVORITE OF MARY

When our dearly beloved Saint was about ten years of age, she fell grievously sick, so much so, that it seemed as though God was going to take her to Himself. She suffered greatly, and as the days went by, her anguish increased. She sometimes remained in the state of extreme exhaustion for hours altogether and in an extraordinary torpor. She tells us that the devil filled her with fears. She was afraid of everything. Her bed seemed to be surrounded by frightful precipices. Nails in the wall took the terrifying appearance of long fingers, shrivelled and blackened with fire, that made her cry out in terror. One day, her good father stood looking at her in silence, hat in hand, when suddenly, it was transformed into some horrible shape, and she was so frightened that the poor man went away sobbing. Of her illness, St. Therese says: "The sickness with which I was attacked certainly came from the jealousy of the devil, who furious at this first entry into Carmel, wished to avenge himself on me for the great harm that my family was to do him in the future. But he did not know that the Queen of Heaven watched faithfully over her little flower, that she smiled upon her from above, and that she hastened to make the tempest stop at the moment when its delicate and fragile stalk was about to be broken once and for all." (p. 44)

The statue of which St. Therese speaks, twice appeared as if endowed with life, in order to console Mme. Martin, the mother of Therese. In later years, when her superior asked her to write the story of her soul, she knelt before this same statue. "As I knelt," she says, "I begged of that dear Mother to guide my hand, and thus ensure that only what was pleasing to her should find place here." That our dear Mother did guide the hand of Little Therese is evidenced by the inspiring words that she has left us as a perpetual memorial of the goodness of God.

The Little Flower well understood that all graces come to us through the mercy of Mary. For whatever is good, whatever sweet, whatever of joy, whatever of grace, must pass through the hands of Mary. God so wills it. Grace was given to St. Therese in such abundance, that when Pope Benedict XV spoke on her heroic virtue, he said in part: "So rich was she in the science of the Saints that she was able to point out to them the true path of salvation. . . . Whence was derived this vast treasure of knowledge? From the secrets which God reveals to little ones."

At the sermons of her Canonization, it was said: "Above all, she nourished her heart and soul with the inspired word of God, on which she meditated continually, and the Spirit of Truth taught her what He hides as a rule from the wise and prudent and reveals to the humble. Indeed God enriched her with a quite exceptional wisdom, so that she was enabled to trace out for others a sure way of salvation."

On reading the letters and autobiography of our beloved Saint, how many sweet passages are addressed to the Blessed Virgin Mary. They are replete with tenderest love, utmost confidence, delicate intimacies. At one time, she says: "But, good Blessed Virgin, it seems to me that I am more fortunate than you, for I have you for a Mother and you have no Blessed Virgin to love." At another: "I hope the Blessed Virgin is filling you to overflowing with her graces; if they are not graces of consolation, they are assuredly graces of light!" "And the Blessed Virgin? Ah! Celine. hide yourself in the shadow of her virginal mantle that she may virginize you. Purity is so lovely, so white! 'Blessed are the pure of heart, for they shall see God.' Yes, they shall see Him even upon earth, where nothing is pure, but where all creatures grow limpid when we look at them with the Face of the loveliest and whitest of Lilies between!" (Letter of 1890)

But to try to cull all the gracious thoughts of St. Therese on Our Blessed Mother is like cutting flowers off the plant, and expecting to retain their full freshness and loveliness in a vase. They can best be appreciated in their natural state. Even so the loving words uttered by the Little Flower, are most enjoyed and give fuller inspiration when read in her writings.

PRAYER

My dearest sister, little Therese, you have found Mary and loved her. And through her, you have found Jesus, our Lord. You loved our Blessed Mother so ardently, that you could truly say that she was your very heart, your soul, your rest, your consolation, your delight, your Mother, and after the Most Adorable Trinity and Jesus most beloved, your All! St. Therese, implore Mary to take me to her heart. May the touch of her hand transform me into the Saint that Jesus wishes me to be. Amen.

DEVOTED CHILD OF ST. JOSEPH

When the Little Flower's heart was drawn to Jesus and Mary, she also sought the embrace of good St. Joseph. She loved St. Joseph, the Foster Father of Jesus, and the chaste spouse of the Blessed Virgin Mary. Thoughts on the Holy Family lifted her soul to God.

She says: "When I picture the Holy Family, the thought that does me most good is—the simplicity of their home-life. Our Lady and St. Joseph were well aware that Jesus was God, while at the same time greater wonders were hidden from them, and—like us—they lived by faith. You have heard those words of the Gospel: 'They understood not the word that He spoke unto them;' and those others no less mysterious: 'His Father and Mother were wondering at those things which were spoken concerning Him.' They seemed to be learning something new, for this word 'wondering' implies a certain amount of surprise."

When Little Therese was questioned as to her methods of sanctifying meals, she answered:

"In the refectory, we have but one thing to do: perform this lowly action with lofty thoughts. I confess that it is often in the refectory that the sweetest aspirations of love come to me. Sometimes I am forced to stop on thinking that if our Lord were in my place, faced with the portions that are served me, He would certainly partake of them. It is very likely that during His mortal life, He tasted the same foods. He ate bread and fruit.

"Here are my childish rubrics:

"I imagine myself in the house of the Holy Family. If I am served, for example, salad, cold fish, wine or something else that has a strong taste, I offer it to good St. Joseph. To the Holy Virgin I give the hot portions, the well-ripened fruit, etc. The portions on festive days, especially boiled beef, rice, jam, I offer to the Child Jesus. Finally, when I am given a distasteful meal, I say to myself gaily: Today, my little one, it is all for you!" (p. 276)

Just as the Sacred Scriptures speak but briefly on good St. Joseph, in like manner, we find that St. Therese dwelt most on her love of Jesus. But that she was tenderly devoted to him is seen in the occasional lines in her writings. She speaks of St. Joseph's labors; she meditates on his heart-aches when the only refuge he could find for the Mother and Child was a crude cave to shelter animals; she dwells on the peace and sanctity of the Holy Family;

and she touches on his manliness, when she sweetly offered him salad, cold fish and wine. It is evident that she spoke familiarly and intimately with dear St. Joseph. Like Teresa of Avila, the Little Flower was a devoted Child of St. Joseph.

Prayer

O St. Therese, devoted child of St. Joseph, teach me how to meditate on the virtues of good St. Joseph. May those meditations cause a holy fire to spring up in my breast, so that I may imitate his goodness and be fully devoted to our sweet Mother Mary and to Jesus, her Son. May I bring the joy and sanctity that St. Joseph brought to the Holy Family into every home and dwelling place I enter. All about him were bettered by his presence. May I, too, draw all hearts to Jesus and Mary, in imitation of St. Joseph.

And, dear St. Joseph, so beloved of the Adorable Trinity, that you were destined from all eternity to be the Spouse of the Mother of God and the Foster Father of the Word made Flesh, open my eyes that I may see how to copy your virtues. In your soul was mirrored the perfection of Jesus and Mary. Look down upon me in pity. Plead for me before the throne of God, that I may obtain the blessing of my Creator, the kiss of my Jesus, and the motherly care of Mary. Amen.

BELOVED DAUGHTER OF ST. TERESA
AND FAITHFUL FOLLOWER OF
ST. JOHN OF THE CROSS

God, in His tender mercy, has given us Saints
to inspire us on our road to Heaven. By word and
example, they teach us to know, love and serve God.
By copying their bright examples, we, too, can become Saints. On reading the writings of St. Therese,
we see how certain Saints uplifted her soul to the
embrace of the Eternal God. She speaks of a number
of Saints. But two in particular, influenced her holy
life: her great mother, St. Teresa of Avila, and
St. John of the Cross. Enlightened by God, she understood their lofty teachings. And it has been her
mission to teach us what she learned, in language
that all souls can understand. The sweet spirit of
St. John of the Cross and the profound sanctity of
St. Teresa of Avila, fill the pages of the Little
Flower's writings.

In the first paragraph of the history of her soul,
St. Therese tells us that she will begin by singing
what must be her eternal song, the "Mercies of the
Lord." And she went on to say: "The flower that

is going to tell her story, rejoices in having to make known the wholly undeserved favors of Jesus." (p. 7)

In revealing all the good things God had done for her, Little Therese was carrying out the spirit of St. Teresa of Avila, who once said: "Let those souls who have reached perfect union with God hold themselves in high esteem, with a humble and holy presumption. Let them keep unceasingly before their eyes the remembrance of the good things they have received; and beware of the thought that they are practising humility in not recognizing the gifts of God. Is it not clear that the constant remembrance of gifts bestowed serves to increase the love for the giver? How can he who ignores the riches he possesses, spend them generously on others?"

Our beloved Saint spent the riches she had on us, and prayed as follows:

"O Jesus! Would that I could tell all little souls of Your ineffable condescension! I feel that if by any possibility You could find one weaker than my own, You would take delight in loading her with still greater favors, provided she abandoned herself with entire confidence to Your infinite mercy. But, O my Beloved, why these desires of mine to make known the secrets of Your love? Is it not You alone who has taught them to me, and can You not reveal them to others? Yes! I know it, and this I implore You to do. I entreat You to let Your divine eyes rest upon a vast number of little souls. I entreat You to choose in this world, a legion of little victims worthy of Your love." (p. 221)

On meditating on the words of St. John of the Cross, St. Therese learned much. She sang with her holy Father, St. John of the Cross:

"In humbling myself so low, so low,
I lifted myself so high, so high,
That I was able to reach my goal!" (p. 262)

The only way to advance rapidly in the path of love, is to remain always little. The Little Flower teaches us that we become true lovers of Jesus by becoming tiny and hidden from the eyes of men. By becoming small, we become great; and in this greatness, we can overtake the Prey we chase— Jesus, the Lover of our souls!

Like St. John of the Cross, our beloved Saint's heart was pierced with arrows of love, the more she heard His goodness spoken of. Her wounds of love increased. Her desires became more ardent. And in this ardor she cried out with her Holy Father:

"Henceforth no more messages send,
Who know not how to tell me what I long to know.
All those who concern themselves with You, without
    exception,

Continually speak to me of Your thousand charms
And wound me still more.
And above all, those who only stammer, cause me to die
In a manner I cannot explain." (p. 296)

Like St. John of the Cross, St. Therese no longer was anxious for things of earth, once she had tasted of love. She gave all her wealth to Jesus. She made all things subservient to love. Her soul was caught in the flame of divine love. With this Saint, she was able to say:

"Inside the cellar of my Beloved, I drank,
And when I came out,
In all this plain
I no longer knew a thing,
And I lost the flock
That I formerly tended.

"My soul busys itself
With all its wealth in His service!
I no longer guard the flock,
I have no other office
For now all my duty is to love.

And she was able to add:

"Since I have experienced it,
Love is so powerful in its results
That it knows how to draw profit from all,

From the good and evil it finds in me,
And transforms my soul into its own." (p. 145)

Speaking of Celine and herself, our dear Saint said: "The burning sparks that he (Jesus) scattered in our souls, the delicious, strong wine which He gave us to drink, made all transitory things here below vanish from our eyes. And from our lips we breathed aspirations of love." (p. 79)

PRAYER

My dearest, Little Sister, beloved of St. Teresa and faithful follower of St. John of the Cross, fill me with the sweetness that possessed your soul. By becoming as small as a grain of sand, I shall be able to reach and embrace my Jesus. By yielding all earthly riches and totally abandoning myself to Jesus, I can attain the sole desire of my soul, complete union with my God. I wish to become a little victim of Divine Love. Have pity on me, my sweet Sister, and draw me on the way of perfection. Amen.

CHILD OF PREDILECTION
FROM THY INFANCY

When we say that our beloved Sister was a "Child of Predilection" from her infancy, we mean that God loved her with a special love. This love, which began from the dawn of her reason, continued to grow throughout her lifetime. And, finally, she gave her beautiful soul back to God, totally consumed as a victim of Divine Love.

God so loved the Little Flower that He awakened her intelligence at an early age, and through the promptings of His divine grace, drew her angelic soul to Himself. She was of an affectionate nature, and returned love for love. But in giving herself to the good God, she did so with the full capacity of love that was granted her by the Divine Mercy.

Her saintly parents taught her to know God. And once she knew Him, she loved Him utterly. Even as a two-year-old baby, just learning to talk, she was offering her soul to the divine Spouse of

Virgins. Years later, the following conversation took place between Little Therese and a soul that cherished her:

"Truly, you are a saint!"

"No, I am not a saint. I have never done the deeds of the saints. I am a very little soul that the good God has laden with graces. In heaven you will see that I say the truth."

"But you have always been faithful to the divine graces, haven't you?"

"Yes, from the age of three, I have refused the good God nothing. Nevertheless, I cannot glorify myself. See how this evening the setting sun colors the tree tops in gold. Even so my soul seems very bright and gilded to you, since it is exposed to the rays of love. But if the divine sun were no longer to send me its fires, I would immediately become obscure and dark." (p. 266)

We know that the soul of our beloved Sister was constantly and most intimately united to God, even from infancy. Her dearly beloved mother bore witness to this, when she wrote to her daughter, Pauline, saying of Little Therese: "The dear little thing is our joy. She will be good, you see the germ of it already: she talks only of the good God; not for the whole world would she miss saying her prayers. I wish you could hear her telling little stories. I have never seen anything so pretty. She makes up for herself the tone and expression that are required."

But our dear Saint's holiness in no way changed her childhood's pleasures. She deeply loved her mother and idolized her good father. As a child, she laughed so heartily that she started others laughing with her. Just like other children of other ages, she enjoyed blowing bubbles; she loved to be held by the hand as she threw back her head and looked at the stars. She looked forward to picnics and felt sorry to see them end. She delighted in flowers. She was happy to walk in the rain. She had daring, once stooping down and walking under the belly of a horse as it blocked her passage. She loved animals and in the course of time, had as pets, a little bird, two chickens and even a baby lamb.

Outwardly, St. Therese seemed as ordinary as any other child. But God had marked her for His own with a special mission in life. And that mission was to teach us of the mercy and the love of God. Little Therese tells us: "And because I was little and weak, He stooped towards me and sweetly instructed me in the secrets of his love." (p. 81) Those secrets, our sweet Sister, Therese, has revealed in her precious writings.

PRAYER

My dearest little Sister Therese, God so loved you that He willed that you love Him from earliest infancy. He enlightened your intellect, that you might know Him. He captivated your will, that you might love Him. You returned love for love. When once you were told what was right and good, you always accepted it and acted accordingly. And at the close of life, you were able to give glory to God by saying that from the age of three you had denied the good God nothing. All through life, you remained a child in the sweetness of virtues. You did not wish to become big, for a child is more easily taken up into one's arms and embraced. A child does not have to provide for itself, for its parents take care of him. Remaining little, my dearest Sister, God carried you close to His Heart. He took care of all your needs. He overwhelmed you with His graces and the tenderest marks of love.

Little Therese, you assure me that if God could find a soul weaker than your own, He would take delight in loading it with still greater favors, provided that she abandon herself with entire confidence to the Infinite Mercy. My soul is weaker than yours, my dearly beloved Therese! But teach me to abandon myself entirely to the Divine Mercy, so that God may take full possession of me!

ANGEL OF THE CLOISTER

The lovely word "angel" is understood to mean a variety of things, and the sense changes with each different interpretation. In one instance, "angel" means a messenger of God. In another, it is understood to designate one who is a guardian. In still other cases, it is an exemplar of virtue to be followed. Again, it could mean one possessing all sweetness and goodness, gifts granted by the Holy Spirit. In what sense, then, is our beloved Little Therese to be understood as the "Angel of the Cloister?"

St. Therese is indeed a messenger of God. From her lips, have come words of wisdom. Her words are like so many jewels, each resplendent with celestial light. In her own gentle way, she teaches us of the mercy and love of God. The lessons she teaches are not new doctrine, only a new presentation. For all that St. Therese taught can be found in the sacred treasury of the Church and in the Holy Scriptures. But God willed that through this sweet maiden, the message of His love should be placed before us once again. In an age when the word "love" has been so falsely represented, God has deigned to give us one who teaches and speaks of "true love" that is compelling and attractive.

Our beloved Saint is a guardian of the Cloister. During her lifetime, she zealously watched over the souls entrusted to her care, forming in them, the image of Jesus Christ. Of this matter, the Little Flower tells us: "You have desired that I carry out at your side, a mission that is very sweet and very easy, and this mission I will complete from on high in heaven. You have said to me as Jesus said to St. Peter, 'Feed my lambs.' And I, I was astonished. I found myself too little and I begged you to graze your little lambs yourself and in your kindness to watch over me with them. Complying somewhat with my just desire, you named me their first companion rather than their mistress, commanding me, nevertheless, to lead them to fertile and shady pastures, to point out to them the best and most nourishing herbs, to name the brilliant but poisonous flowers which they must never touch except to crush underfoot. How is it, Mother, that my youth and inexperience did not frighten you at all? How is it that you were not afraid that I would lead your lambs astray? In so acting, perhaps you recalled that the Lord is often pleased to give his wisdom to little ones." (p. 155) Just as our beloved Sister watched over the cloister while she yet walked this earth, she will still continue to do so, from her abode in Heaven. She has given us her word. She will not break it.

The Little Flower is an example to be followed. She was a perfect religious, as her actions testify. Speaking of the joy of religious obedience, our dear Saint says: "My God, from what disquiet one delivers oneself by taking the vow of obedience! How happy are simple religious! Their only compass being the will of their superiors, they are always assured that they are on the right road, not having to be afraid that they are making a mistake, even if it seems certain to them that their superiors are mistaken. But as soon as they cease to consult the infallible compass, immediately the soul wanders down arid roads where the water of grace is soon lacking to them. Mother, you are the compass that Jesus has given me to guide me surely to the eternal shore. How sweet it is for me to fix my gaze on you and then to accomplish the will of the Lord! In permitting me to suffer temptations against faith, the divine Master has greatly increased within my heart the spirit of faith, which He has me see living in your soul and communicating to me His blessed commands." (p. 164) If all religious were to follow the example of this dear Saint, to what great heights of sanctity they would attain.

Our beloved Sister was an angel of sweetness, goodness and mercy, to all with whom she came in contact. She was constantly thoughtful of others. Her disposition was ever cheerful, even in her greatest sufferings. She treated all her companions, even as she would treat Our Lord Jesus Christ. No greater praise can be given her than that. For it is another way of saying that perfect charity reigned within her soul.

In imitation of our beloved Saint, we too, can be "angels." We can be messengers of God, His mouthpieces, by the words we use, the counsel we give. We can be guardians of virtuous life and can inspire others to do good by our examples. And with love of neighbor reigning in our soul, we can be as an Angel of sweetness, goodness and mercy, to all with whom we come in contact.

PRAYER

My dearest St. Therese, so justly called the Angel of the Cloister, inspire me with efficacious resolutions to imitate you. For by so doing, I will draw my soul closer to the God of Love and lead others to do the same. Plead for me, that perfect charity reign within my soul. For with perfect, divine love, I will truly live and breathe in the embrace of my God. Little Therese, pray for me.

SERAPH OF THE ALTAR

How ardently St. Therese loved Jesus in the Most Blessed Sacrament is seen in the words she penned. In her Act of Oblation as a victim of Divine Love, she prayed as follows: Her Divine Son, my beloved Spouse, during the days of His mortal life said to us: 'If you ask the Father anything in My name, He will give it to you.' (John 16:23) I am certain, then, that You will fulfill my desires. I know, O my God, the more You wish to give, the more You make us desire. Within my heart I feel immense desires, and it is with confidence that I ask You to come and take possession of my soul. Ah! I cannot receive Holy Communion as often as I desire. But, Lord, are You not All-Powerful? Remain within me as in the Tabernacle, never leave Your liitle victim. I would console You for the ingratitude of the wicked. And I beg You to take away from me the liberty of being able to displease You. If through weakness I sometimes fall, may Your divine gaze immediately purfiy my soul, consuming all my imperfections, just as fire transforms everything into itself." (p. 305)

In a letter she wrote to her cousin, Marie Guerin, she reveals the ardor of her love, when she exhorts her saying: "Marie of the Blessed Sacrament . . . your name tells you your mission. To console Jesus, to get souls to love Him . . . Jesus is sick for love, and one must realize that 'the sickness of love is cured by love.' . . . Marie, give all your heart to Jesus, He is athirst for it, hungry for it; your heart, to have that is His ambition—so much so that to have it for Himself He consents to dwell in a dark and unclean corner. . . . Ah! How can we fail to love a Friend Who reduces Himself to such utter destitution." (Letter of July, 1890)

And in the same month and year, she wrote to her soul's echo, her dearest Celine, saying: "Let us make a little tabernacle in our hearts where Jesus can find refuge, then He will be consoled, and He will forget what we cannot forget—the ingratitude of souls who leave Him alone in a deserted tabernacle."

On meditating on the Last Supper, St. Therese's soul burned to imitate Jesus in the love He had for the children of God. He gave His new Commandment in telling His Apostles to love one another as He had loved them. St. Therese goes on to say: "I set out to find out how Jesus had loved His disciples. I saw that it was not for their natural qualities. I had ascertained that they were ignorant and full of earthly thoughts. (p. 165) Then she prayed as follows: "O my Jesus! I know that You do not command anything that is impossible. You know my weakness and my imperfection. You well know that I can never arrive to loving my sisters as You love them, if You, O my divine Savior, do not love them in me. It is because You wish to grant me this grace that You have made a new commandment. Oh! How I love it! since it gives me the assurance that it is Your will to love in me all those You command me to love." (p. 166) One of the fruits of receiving Jesus in the Most Blessed Sacrament is a greater love of neighbor. How beautiful and consoling is the truth expressed by our beloved Saint when she said: "Yes, I feel it, when I am charitable, it is Jesus alone Who is acting within me. The more I am united to Him, the more also I love all my sisters." (p. 167)

In her "Canticle of Love," our sweet seraph, Therese, speaks intimately with Jesus, crying out: "The vocation of a Priest! With what love, my Jesus, would I bear Thee in my hand, when my words brought Thee down from Heaven! With what love would I give Thee to souls! And yet while longing to be a Priest, I admire and envy the humility of St. Francis of Assisi, and am drawn to imitate him by refusing the sublime dignity of the Priesthood. How reconcile these opposite tendencies?"

Our beloved Saint gave expression to her love for the Most Blessed Sacrament, in her poem entitled "I Thirst for Love." She says in part:

"You, the great God that the universe adores,
Live within me, a prisoner night and day.
At every hour, Your sweet voice implores
And You tell me over and over: I thirst! I thirst for love!

I, too, am Your prisoner
And on my turn I would repeat
Your tender and divine prayer,
My Beloved, my Brother:
I thirst for love!

I thirst for love! Fulfill my hope.
Increase within me, O Lord, Your divine fire!
I thirst for love! How great is my suffering.
Ah! I would fly to You my God!

Your love is my only martyrdom.
The more I feel it burn within me,
The more my soul desires You.

O Jesus, grant that I may die
For love of You!" (p. 399)

PRAYER

My sweetest Sister, Little Therese, I long to love Jesus
with all my soul. I adore Him from the abyss of my nothingness
I yield myself entirely to Him. O Therese, plead with the Holy
Spirit to inspire me with divine love, to give me the grace to
love Jesus as I ought. My dearest Sister, Therese, ask Mary,
our lovely Blessed Mother, to give me a share in her love for
Jesus. My Jesus in the Most Blessed Sacrament, I love you.

MOST PERFECT RELIGIOUS

A perfect religious is one who yields herself completely and utterly to the love of Jesus. She lives only for Jesus. She wishes to be forgotten by creatures. She seeks only the glory of her divine Spouse. For love of Him, she joyfully accepts whatever befalls her, both good and evil. She is no longer her own, for she is entirely possessed by Jesus, the Heavenly Lover. Such a one was St. Therese of the Child Jesus. Her desires and actions give witness of this.

As a religious, our beloved Saint knew that she did not enter the religious life to seek personal comfort and consolations. She came to give Jesus all her love. Read her words to Sister Agnes of Jesus, wherein she says: "My soul is still in the underground tunnel but it is very happy there, yes, happy to have no consolation, for thus I see that its love is not like the love of the world's brides who are always looking at their bridegrooms' hands to see if they bear a gift, or at his face in the hope of a surprising smile of love to enchant them. . . . But Jesus' poor bride feels that she loves Jesus for Himself alone, and wishes to look upon the face of her Beloved only for a sudden glimpse of the tears which flow from eyes that have enchanted her with their hidden charms! . . . She wants to gather up these tears, to adorn herself with them on the day of her marriage. This adornment too will be hidden, but the Beloved will know it for what it is."

How perfectly the will of St. Therese was united to the Divine Will is evidenced when she tells us: "Let us not refuse Him the least sacrifice; everything is so big in religion. . . . To pick up a pin through love could convert a soul! How mysterious it is! Ah! only Jesus can give such a value to our acts, so let us love Him with all our might." (Letter of May 1894)

The heart of a religious must be emptied of all earthly attachments. It must be willing to serve Jesus for Himself alone, and not for the consolation He gives her. . . . The heart of the religious should find happiness in knowing that the good God, the whole Trinity, gazes upon her, that It is within her and rejoices to be dwelling within her soul.

St. Therese teaches us: "How shall we sing the songs of Sion in a strange land? For long have we hung up our harps on the willows by the river, for we cannot play them! . . . Our God, our heart's

Guest knows it well, so He comes within us in the intent of finding a dwelling place, an *empty* tent, in the midst of the world's battlefield. He asks no more than that, and He is Himself the divine Musician Who is responsible for the harmony. Ah! if we could hear that unutterable harmony, if one single vibration could reach our ears!" (Letter of July 1894).

The religious understands well that we have only the brief instant of life, that we can give to God. It is her happiness to suffer for Him Who loves her even unto folly, and to pass for a fool in the eyes of the world.

Jesus was charged as mad by Herod. But it was a madness of love! True, it was folly to seek the poor, little hearts of mortals to make them His thrones, He the King of Glory, Who is throned above the Cherubim! He Whose presence is mightier than the Heavens can contain! Jesus was mad to come down to earth seeking sinners to make them His friends, His intimates, to make them like unto Himself, when He was perfectly happy with the two adorable Persons of the Trinity! As dear St. Therese comments: "We shall never be able to commit the follies for Him that He has committed for us, nor do our actions deserve the name folly, for they are in fact most reasonable acts, far below what our love would like to accomplish. So that it is the world which is backward, not realizing what

Jesus has done to save it. It is the world which is the all-devouring thing, seducing souls and leading them to fountains without water. . . . Nor are we the lazy, the thriftless ones. Jesus defended us, in the person of Magdalen." (Letter of August 1894)

By keeping the Rule of Carmel to the best of her ability, Little Therese saved her soul. She became the great Saint she is. In like manner, all religious who keep the Holy Rule they have embraced by the vows of religion, can do the same.

PRAYER

Dear St. Therese, perfect model for all religious to imitate, pray that all those who have consecrated themselves to God may follow you with simplicity of heart. In your life, you have done all things sweetly and without much ado. The goal before you was one: Love of God. Implore the Divine Majesty to look with favorable eye upon His religious; that He stir up the graces within their soul; that they become other Little Flowers, to gladden His divine eyes.

ABANDONED TO THE WILL OF GOD

What is meant by abandonment to the Will of God? Abandonment to the Will of God means that out of love for God, the soul embraces all that befalls it, whether of good or of evil, and sees in all things either the direct Will of God or His permissive Will.

What is the direct Will of God? The direct Will of God embraces all those things God causes to take place and finds complacence in their performance. It is the direct Will of God that the plants in the fields grow. Storms and days of calm are all the direct Will of God. So, too, are many of the things that come upon us personally. We are granted certain gifts of body and soul and mind, according to the direct Will of God.

However, the permissive Will of God means that God does not directly will a certain action to take place, but He permits it. Nothing can take place, unless God wills it. But there are certain things that God merely permits to take place, because He has granted man free will. God does cooperate in the action, or it could not be placed. But God is displeased with the human agent placing the action. Only God's permissive Will is in the action. Examples of this may be found in crimes committed by men. When a man steals from his neighbor, he could not walk or lift a finger, unless God gave him power to move. But God does not directly will what the man is doing of wrong. Yet, He does permit it, or the man could not take even the initial step.

Sanctity is found in embracing all that comes upon one, whether it is because of the direct Will of God, or because of the permissive Will of God.

When the soul embraces all in such a spirit, it is truly abandoned to the Will of God.

To accept all that befalls you, whether good or evil, as coming from the direct or permissive Will of God, will sanctify you. It is a known truth expressed by philosophers, that: *Omne Ens Bonum est Hominibus*. Translated, it simply means that no matter what happens to us, we can use it to our good. You must recall that you can be benefited physically or spiritually. Sometimes, the betterments are both for physical and spiritual good. There are other times when what is physically good, may be spiritually harmful. Pleasures that are illicit and sinful can wreak harm upon the soul, even though they cause bodily well-being. At other times, what is spiritually good, may be physically distasteful. An example of this is to accept humiliations for the love of God. Another example would be the death of a loved one. The loss of the beloved causes anguish, but can be the means of drawing the soul closer to Almighty God.

By practicing abandonment to the Will of God, you will experience peace of mind and soul, and as much happiness as may be allotted to man in this life. For then nothing casts you down. Joy or sorrow, riches or poverty, praise or ridicule, nothing will disturb the soul. Since all comes from the loving hand of God, all is equally good and equally sweet. It is by abandonment to the Will of God that you will become a saint.

You must not think that you can reach perfect abandonment to the Will of God with great ease. While it is true that God can do all within the twinkling of an eye, in the usual course of things God desires that you cooperate with the graces He gives you. Each grace is a stepping stone that will enable you to reach the haven of complete abandonment. On this matter, our beloved Little Therese says: "I must confess that my soul was far from mature. I had to pass through many trials before reaching the shore of peace, before tasting the delicious fruits of total abandonment and perfect love." (p. 43)

The Death of St. Therese –E. Giaroli

"I would not want to suffer less!" Looking at her crucifix, Therese said, "Oh! I love Him! My God, I . . . love You!"

Such a wonderful thing is complete abandonment to the Will of God, that St. Therese tells us: "It would need a tongue not of this earth to express the beauty of total abandonment of a heart in Jesus' hands; my heart could do no more than stammer what it felt. . . ."

At first, you may find it difficult to truly abandon yourself to the Will of God. But you will find that once you have sweetly yielded yourself to God in this way, a joy surpassing all previous joys will be yours. You will delight in the embrace of God!

It must be understood that when one completely abandons himself to the Will of God, he is acting in a rational manner. God has given him an intellect, and so he understands the events that take place in his life. He has given him a will to freely embrace all that comes from the hands of God. While embracing the Will of God, he knows that he must do all that he can to better himself, help himself. But at the same time, he accepts God's Will as made known to him.

Prayer

My dearest little Therese, so childlike in your total abandonment to the Will of God, pray that I may imitate you in this. For so doing, I will delight the Heart of God, and will be able to attain a happy eternity. My adorable Trinity, I abandon myself entirely to You in all things. O grant me the graces I need to live in constant union with Your sweet Will. Little Therese, beloved child of God, pray for me.

FORTRESS OF TRUST AND CONFIDENCE

Because St. Therese understood so well what is meant by God's mercy, she became a fortress of trust and confidence in His Divine Will. Well did she know, that to show mercy, is to give your heart to the wretched and miserable. The more wretched our condition, the more is God inclined to show us His love and pity. And the soul, overwhelmed in the tender embrace of God, delights in absolute trust and confidence in the goodness of the Creator.

When suffering and anguish of soul came upon her, so much the more did St. Therese increase in trust and confidence in Jesus. All suffering was a means to draw her own soul, and the souls of others, to Jesus Who suffered such bitter anguish for love of us. It helps so much, when one is suffering, to have loving hearts echo back our grief. Jesus is suffering much, for the love He bears us is not being repaid by love. Because of this, Little Therese wrote: "The song of suffering in union with His sufferings is what most delights His heart . . . Jesus burns with love for

us—look at His adorable Face . . . Look at His glazed
and sunken eyes! . . . Look at His wounds . . . Look
Jesus in the face! . . . There, you will see how He
loves us." (Letter of April 1889). And in a letter
written a month before this, our beloved Saint tells
us: "Let us offer our sufferings to Jesus to save souls;
poor souls! . . . they have fewer graces than we, yet
all the blood of a God has been shed to save them . . .
Jesus has chosen to make their salvation depend on
a sigh of our heart. What a mystery is there! . . . If a
sigh can save a soul, what cannot sufferings like ours
do? . . . Let us refuse Jesus nothing!"

How sad it is, that some lose trust and confidence in God, when He enriches them with suffering. Holiness does not lie in saying beautiful things,
or even in thinking them or feeling them, St. Therese
teaches. It lies in truly willing to suffer. How strongly the Little Flower words this: "Sanctity! it has to
be won at the point of the sword, one must suffer
. . . agonize!" (Letter of April 1888) When suffering
is our lot, our trust and confidence in God should
grow, for He is giving us great testimonies of
His love.

Others grow cold in their trust in God, when
they find themselves humanly weak and full of
faults. After falling into errors for a time, they no
longer strive to increase in divine love. They do not
draw close to the bosom of God, but lag behind, and

seemingly wish to hide from His gaze. Some even remorselessly plunge into more faults, deceiving themselves into believing that there is nothing good they can do; that God is no longer interested in their salvation. How unlike St. Therese are those souls!

The Little Flower compares herself to a little bird. The little bird is distracted a little from its sole business of loving God. It takes a grain on this side or that, runs after a worm . . . again, it finds a little pool of water and wets its barely formed plumage. It sees a flower that pleases it, and its little mind is occupied about the flower. In a word, not being able to soar like the eagles, the poor little bird still bothers with the trifles of this earth. Then, Little Therese goes on to say: "But even now, after all its misdeeds, the little bird doesn't go and hide in a corner to bewail its wretchedness and die of contrition, but turns to the Sun, its Beloved, presents its wet wings, and cries like the swallow; and in its sweet song, it confides its infidelities, tells them in detail, thinking, in the audacity of its total trust, to win in greater plenitude the love of Him 'who came not to call the just but sinners.' (Matt. 9:13) If the adored Star remains deaf to the plaintive twitter of its little creature, if it remains veiled by cloud . . . in that event, the little creature stays wet, it accepts to be numb with cold, and rejoices in the suffering which of course it has deserved." (14 Sept. 1896)

Little Therese, on various occasions, told us that you cannot be half a saint. You must be a whole saint or no saint at all. To become a saint, we must have confidence in God. We must be daring in our love. Consider Mary Magdalen. She comes forward in the face of a crowd of guests, and waters with her tears the feet of her adored Master. As she touched Him for the first time, she must have realized in her heart, the fathomless depths of love and mercy in Jesus' Heart. She realized this, despite her sins. She understood that the Sacred Heart was ready not only to pardon her, but actually to lavish on her the treasures of His divine intimacy, and raise her to the highest summits of contemplation.

Ponder on the words of our beloved Saint, who says: "Since it has been given me too to realize the love of Jesus' Heart, I own that it has driven from my own heart all fear! The remembrance of my faults humiliates me, leads me never to rely on my strength, which is only weakness; but the remembrance speaks to me still more of mercy and love. When one casts one's faults into the consuming flame of Love, how could they fail to be consumed past return?" (Letter June 1897)

Prayer

My sweet little Sister, how patiently and tenderly you instruct me to have absolute confidence and trust in Jesus. How can I ever thank God, for having taken full possession of you and used you as an instrument of His love, to teach me! Help me on my way to Heaven, my dear Sister. When through human weakness I do not have that full confidence and trust in God that I should have, oh, do stir up the graces God has given me. Pray that my mind may be enlightened. Plead with God that He take me by the hand.

POOR IN DESIRES

On reading the inspiring writings of St. Therese, one cannot help but note that her soul was filled with ardent desires. How, then, can she be said to be poor in desires? What is meant by "poor in desires?" In answer to those questions, let us read the letter our beloved Saint wrote on September 17, 1896, to Sister Marie of the Sacred Heart. She writes as follows:

"My dearest Sister,

I am not embarrassed to answer you. . . . How can you ask me if it is possible for you to love the good God as I love Him? . . . If you had understood the story of my little bird, you would not ask me such a question. My desires for martyrdom are nothing, it is not they that give me the limitless confidence I feel in my heart. In fact they are the spiritual riches which make us unjust—when we rest in them complacently and think they are something great.

"These desires are a consolation that Jesus sometimes grants to weak souls like mine (and such

souls are numerous), but when He does not give
this consolation it is a grace of privilege. Remember
the words of Father: 'Martyrs have suffered with
joy, and the King of Martyrs suffered with sorrow.'

"Yes, Jesus said: 'Father, take away this chalice
from me.' Dearest Sister, after that how can you say
that my desires are the mark of my love? Ah!
I realize that what pleases God in my little soul is
not that. What pleases Him is to see me love my
littleness and poverty, the blind hope I have in His
mercy. . . . That is my sole treasure, dearest God-
mother; why should not this treasure be yours? . . .

"Are you not ready to suffer whatever the good
God wants? I know well that you are; then, if you
want to feel joy in suffering, to be drawn to it, what
you seek is your own consolation, for when one loves
a thing, the pain vanishes. I assure you that if we
went together to martyrdom in the dispositions in
which we now are, you would have great merit and
I none, unless it pleased Jesus to change my dispositions.

"O my dearest Sister, please understand your
little sister, understand that to love Jesus, to be His
victim of love, the weaker one is, without desires
or virtues, the more apt one is for the operations of
that consuming and transforming love. The desire
to be a victim is enough of itself, but one must consent to stay always poor and without strength, and

that's the difficulty, for where are we to find the man truly poor in spirit? He must be sought afar, says the psalmist. He does not say we must look for him among great souls, but 'afar,' that is in lowliness, nothingness. Ah! do let us stay very far from all that is brilliant, let us love our littleness, love to feel nothing, then we shall be poor in spirit, and Jesus will come for us, afar off as we are, He will transform us in love's flames. . . . Oh! how I wish I could make you realize what I mean! . . . It is trust, and nothing but trust, that must bring us to love. . . . Fear brings us only justice. (To strict justice as it is shown to sinners, but that is not the justice Jesus will have for those who love Him.)

"Since we see the way, let us run together. Yes, I feel that Jesus wants to give us Heaven as a free gift. O, my dearest Sister, if you don't understand me, it is because you are too great a soul . . . or rather because I explain myself badly, for I am sure that the good God would not give you the desire to be possessed by Him, by His merciful love, if He did not have this favor in store for you; or rather He has already given it to you since you are given over to Him, since you desire to be consumed by Him, and the good God never gives desires that He cannot fulfill. . . ."

Contained in this letter are the answers to our questions. What is mean by "poor in desires"? To be poor in desires is to love our littleness, love to feel nothing, and to have a blind hope in the mercy of God. In what manner was St. Therese poor in desires? St. Therese was poor in spirit in that she did not rely on the human virtues that God had given her, for her support. She acknowledged those gifts of God. She thanked Him for them. But she leaned entirely upon God Himself for her support.

To be poor in desires is nothing else than to have one goal in mind: to love God and to draw souls to God for the love we bear Him. On this point, our dearly beloved Saint tells us: "There is a verse in the Divine Office which I recite each day with reluctance: ('I have inclined my heart to do Thy justifications forever, because of the reward.') I hasten to add in my heart: 'My Jesus, Thou knowest I do not serve Thee for sake of reward, but solely out of love, and a desire to win Thee souls.'"

To be poor in desires is to have perfect love. To be poor in desires, is to want God to take possession of you in such wise that your actions are no more yours or human, but divine—inspired and guided by the Spirit of love.

To be poor in desires is another way of saying that the soul lives in the embrace of God, and does all in and for and through the Will of the Divine Majesty.

So much can be said on poverty of spirit. But on meditating on the words of our sweet Sister, you may gain much. Do so.

PRAYER

My dear Sister Therese, so poor in spirit that you were truly rich, may I live as you did, with only one goal in view: to love God with all my heart, with all my mind, with all my strength, with all my soul. May I love my neighbor for the love of God, and draw all souls to His divine embrace.

BEAUTIFUL FLOWER OF CARMEL

Love oftentimes prompts the lover to compare his beloved to a beautiful flower, a fragrant flower, whose delicate form and gracious appearance delight his eyes. Nor is this to be marveled at. Christ is sometimes called the Lily of the Valleys, and, at other times, a tender plant growing in a thirsty soil. Our Holy Mother the Church is called a "garden enclosed" by the Divine Spirit. And we are sweetly taught to call upon the Mother of God, as the "Mystical Rose."

St. Therese looked upon the world of souls, and she called it "Our Lord's living garden." She tells us that "So it is in the world of souls, the living garden of the Lord. He has found it good to create great saints who can be compared to lilies and roses. But he has also created the smallest, which must content themselves in being daisies or simple violets destined to gladden His divine eyes when He lowers them to His feet. The happier the flowers are in doing His will, the more perfect they are." (p. 5)

Our dear Saint may be compared to a flower for various reasons. During her lifetime upon earth, and now that she is in Heaven, she still continues to shed sweet perfumes upon the earth. Her written words have the fragrance of Heaven. And in their sweet odor, souls run as giants on the way to perfection.

To flowers we attribute certain qualities. The violet, that loves to grow in secret places and seems to hide its beauty from all eyes, is called "modest." The red rose, so much like the blushing face of a beloved, is made the symbol of "love" and "charity." And the lily, with its spotless whiteness, is the symbol for "purity." St. Therese is indeed a "modest violet of humility," a "sweet rose of charity," and a "fragrant lily of purity."

Modest violet of humility! For love of God, she wished to be hidden from all creatures, and considered as nothing. She tells us: "Trying to be forgotten, I shall wish to be seen by none save Jesus. . . . What matter if I appear poor and totally lacking in intelligence and talent. . . . I want to put into practice this counsel from the Imitation: 'Let this one glory himself for one thing, and that one for another, do you put your joy only in contempt of yourself, in My will and My glory,' or again: 'Do you wish to learn something that may serve you: love to be ignored and counted as nothing!' " (Letter of

April, 1895) What humility our dear Saint had is evident when she refers to herself as a little grain of sand, as a worthless toy, as a tiny paint brush, a little bird. And what resulted from her humility? She felt great peace in her soul. Jesus was satisfied with her ardent desires, with her total abandonment, and drew her closer still to His Sacred Heart.

Sweet rose of charity! St. Therese gives us a veiled glimpse of the heavenly charity that filled her soul, in the words she penned in her Autobiography, now in two chapters known as "The New Commandment" and "A Canticle of Love." To make selections from these two chapters is most difficult, since their entirety carries their heavenly fragrance. She loved Jesus so much that she spoke of Him as follows:

"Love attracts love; mine darts towards You and would want to fill to overflowing the abyss which attracts her. But, alas! It is not even a drop of dew lost in the Ocean! To love You as You love me, I would have to borrow Your own love. Thus alone can I find rest. O my Jesus, it seems to me that You cannot overwhelm a soul with more love than You have poured out on mine, and that is why I dare to ask that You love those You have given me, just as You have loved me." (p. 201) Because she loved God so ardently, she loved her neighbor with an all-embracing love. She loved her neighbor with the same love of Jesus Christ!

Fragrant lily of purity! St. Therese, bride of Christ, spoke as follows, in a letter written in May, 1890: "What a joy for our hearts to remember that our little family loves Jesus so tenderly! That is always my consolation. . . . Surely our family is a virginal family, a family of lilies? Ask Jesus that the smallest and last may not be the last to love Him with all her power of loving." It must not be thought that because St. Therese is a lily of purity, that she was ignorant of the dignity of motherhood. At one time, she tells us: "The loveliest masterpiece of the heart of God is the heart of a mother." And again: "God has poured into the hearts of mothers something of the love with which His own Heart overflows." On the day of Celine's veiling, St. Therese wrote to her sister as follows: "For Him alone will Celine bring forth children; she will water the seeds with her tears, and Jesus will be always joyous, bearing sheaves of lilies in His hands. . . ." St. Therese understood that there is a spiritual fatherhood and a spiritual motherhood, which far surpasses that of the flesh.

Not only is St. Therese a lily of purity because of chastity, she is such also because she possessed all virtues to a perfect degree. She was pure in the sense of possessing perfection. In her whole lifetime, she never committed a mortal sin. She avoided all deliberate, venial sins. She had only to be told what was good, and she ever after strove for it. Little Therese mirrored Our Blessed Mother in purity, a purity which meant having all perfection! Only the degree was different.

Truly may St. Therese be called the beautiful flower of carmel!

PRAYER

My dearest little Sister, possessing so many virtues that you may be called a "garden enclosed," help me to imitate you. The fragrance of all the flowers was found in you. Even so must each soul be imbued, to please the Sacred Heart. I wish to comfort Jesus. I wish to gladden His eyes. Little Therese, may I stay close to you always, so that your fragrance may be with me, and Jesus may look with gracious eye upon me.

PATRONESS OF MISSIONARIES

On December 14, 1927, Pope Pius XI, of blessed memory, published a pontifical decree, declaring St. Therese of the Child Jesus principal patron, with St. Francis Xavier, of all missionaries, both men and women, and of missions throughout the world. Good St. Francis Xavier traveled the face of the earth, to bring the good news of salvation to men. His body was worn out with labors. Hardships of many kinds were his. But the ardor of his love pressed him ever onward, that he might gain more souls to the love of Christ Crucified. He was a missionary in deed and in word. His example is an inspiration to all missionaries, both men and women. His intercession is powerful before the throne of God. But why is Little Therese placed, as it were, on an equal footing with the great Francis Xavier? She was a cloistered nun. She did not sway the thoughts of men during her lifetime on earth, as did St. Catherine of Sienna. She did not appear before the leaders of government or councils of kings. Her voice did not thrill the multitudes. Hers was a hidden life, even from many in her own community in Carmel. Why, then, is she Patroness of Missionaries?

St. Therese is Patroness of Missionaries and Missions, because of the consuming love she had for souls. She wished to save souls, that more love might be given to the good God. In her Canticle of Love, she cries out: "I would want to enlighten souls like the prophets and doctors. I would want to travel the earth to preach Your Name and to plant Your glorious cross on heathen soil, O my Beloved! But one mission would not be enough for me. I would want to announce the Gospel at the same time in all parts of the world, even to the most remote islands. I would want to be a missionary not only for a few years, but I would want to have been so since the creation of the world even to the consummation of the ages. Ah! Above all I would want to be a martyr! A martyr! Behold the dream of my youth; and this dream has grown with me in my little cell at Carmel. But this too is folly, for I do not desire one kind of torment only. To satisfy me, I would have to have them all." (p. 214)

On the feast of the Assumption, 1892, St. Therese wrote in part: "Surely because Jesus has so incomprehensible a love for us, He wants us to have a share with Him in the salvation of souls. He wants to do nothing without us. The Creator of the universe waits for the prayer of a poor little soul to save the souls redeemed like it at the price of His blood. . . . Is not the apostolate of prayer lifted higher, so to speak, than the apostolate of preaching? Our mission, as Carmelites, is to form those Gospel laborers. They will save millions of souls, whose mothers we shall be. . . ." On still another occasion, St. Therese cried out: "Oh! how sweet it is to love Him and to make Him loved!"

St. John of the Cross says: "The smallest movement of pure love is more useful to the Church than all works put together." The soul of St. Therese pressed hungrily towards God, from the dawn of her reason. Just as a child seeks its mother's breast for nourishment, even so did Little Therese, during her entire lifetime, draw closer and closer to the God of Love. There are so many passages in her writings that testify to this. In one of her letters, she says: "Our Lord, wishing my first glance to be for Him alone, deigned to ask me for my heart actually in the cradle, if I may put it so." How many and how fervent were her acts of pure love! And how many souls she drew to God by the sighs of her heart! If the slightest movements of pure love are so useful to the Church, how wondrously did St. Therese enrich the Church, for she added all her sufferings and prayers to the love that overflowed from the chalice of her heart.

Well is St. Therese Patroness of Missionaries and of Missions! Her heart was all enflamed with divine love. She loved God with her whole being. And because she loved the Divine Majesty so much, she also loved all souls redeemed by the Precious Blood of Jesus. She prayed for their salvation. She suffered for their salvation. All this, so that the good God might be loved as He ought!

The goal of all missionaries is to bring souls to the loving embrace of God. Since Little Therese taught us so tenderly of the merciful love of God, it was fitting that she be appointed Patroness of all those men and women who seek to draw souls to the Heart of the Savior.

Immediately after she made that Act of Oblation, on June 9, 1895, Little Therese tells us: "From that day I have been penetrated and surrounded with love. Every moment this merciful love renews me and purifies me, leaving in my soul no trace of sin."

If all souls approach the Divine Majesty with the childlike love and abandonment of St. Therese, they will certainly save their souls. Perhaps that is the reason why Holy Mother the Church has given us St. Therese as Patroness of the Missions and Missionaries!

Prayer

My dear little Sister, Therese, so much in love with God that He was in your thoughts all day, draw me close to the heavenly flame that enkindled your soul. It is through prayer and sacrifice that souls are saved and love proven. May I hunger to suffer and be forgotten, so that I may give glory to God and lead souls to His tender embrace.

ZEALOUS GUARDIAN OF THE CLERGY

The sacred priesthood confers great dignity upon a man. It sets him apart from the rest of men, because of the sublime tasks that are his. He is the mediator between God and men! He is another Christ in deeds. The priest is the minister of God's mercies. Christ comes to us through His priests. He walks about in His priests. Through His priests, Christ goes about the world, teaching, correcting, consoling, sacrificing. Through His priests, Jesus, the Supreme High Priest, renews the holy bonds of charity between the Divine Heart and the heart of men.

But with all his sacred powers, the priest is but a creature. Unless he stir up the graces God has given him in the holy sacrament of Orders, he will become merely a signpost of salvation. He will point out the direction to others, while he himself becomes a castaway. The priest needs prayer. He must pray. And if he neglects to pray as he ought, then others should pray for him. Some are not aware of the spiritual needs of their priests, and seldom pray for them. There are others who look with scorn on the weakness of a priest. And if he is a shepherd who has deserted his flock, some despise him and will not lift a finger to help him. How differently did St. Therese act!

In her Autobiography, she tells us that while on her trip to Rome, she gained much valuable knowledge. What was this knowledge? There were two things she stressed. "I understood," she said, "that true greatness is not found in a name but in the soul. . . . The second experience I had concerned priests. Up until then, I could not understand the principal end of the Carmelite Reform. To pray for sinners ravished me. But to pray for priests whose souls seemed as pure as crystal, that seemed to me astonishing! Ah! I understood my vocation in Italy. It was not too far to go in search of so useful information. During a month, I met many holy priests, and I saw that if their sublime dignity lifted them above the angels, they are none the less weak and fragile. Then if holy priests that Jesus calls the salt of the earth need our prayers, what must we say of those who are lukewarm? Has not our Lord again said: 'But if salt loses its strength, what shall it be salted with?' O Mother, how beautiful is our vocation!" (p. 94)

Note that St. Therese does not condemn the Priests for their weakness. She prays for them! Consider her words, written to her beloved sister, Celine, in July of 1889. She says in part: "Celine, during the brief moments that remain to us, let us not waste our time . . . let us save souls . . . souls 'are lost like snowflakes' and Jesus weeps, and we are thinking only of our own sorrow instead of consoling our Spouse! Oh! my Celine, let us live for souls, let us be apostles, especially let us save the souls of priests, souls which should be more transparent than crystal. . . . Let us pray, let us suffer for them, and on the last day, Jesus will be grateful. We shall give Him souls!"

That October, 1889, she again wrote to Celine saying: "Ah! Celine, I feel that Jesus is asking us to slake His thirst by giving Him souls, souls of priests above all. I feel that Jesus wants me to tell you this, for our mission is to forget ourselves, to annihilate ourselves . . . we are so small a matter . . . yet Jesus wills that the salvation of souls should depend on our sacrifices, our love. He is a beggar begging us for souls . . . ah! let us understand the look on His face! So few can understand it. Jesus does us the marvelous favor of instructing us Himself, showing us a hidden light."

To the Little Flower, a fallen-away priest is a "withered lily that must be changed into a rose of love and repentance" by prayer and sacrifice of those who know him and of those who love him.

St. Therese wished to help priests by prayer and suffering. Now that she is enjoying the bliss of Paradise, she can no longer suffer. But her prayers are constantly before the Face of God, like a sweet incense, constantly interceding for all souls, but priests, in particular.

Join our beloved Saint, in prayer and sacrifice for the clergy. You may be sure that God will reward you abundantly.

Prayer

My little Sister, Therese, so anxious for the holiness of Christ's priests, I thank you for your charity. O continue to pray for them, that the love of God will inflame them. May all priests be clothed in the fiery cloak of love that enkindled you! In that way, how many sparks of love they may scatter throughout the world! Pray, dearly beloved Saint, that Holy Mother the Church be blessed with good priests, priests consumed with zeal for the Will of God and fully imbued with His divine love.

DAUGHTERS OF ST. PAUL

IN MASSACHUSETTS
  50 St. Paul's Ave.
    Jamaica Plain
    Boston, Mass. 02130
  172 Tremont St.
    Boston, Mass. 02111
  381 Dorchester St.
    So. Boston, Mass. 02127
  325 Main St.
    Fitchburg, Mass.
IN NEW YORK
  78 Fort Place
    Staten Island, N.Y. 10301
  625 East 187th St.
    Bronx, N.Y.
  39 Erie St.
    Buffalo, N.Y. 14202
IN CONNECTICUT
  202 Fairfield Ave.
    Bridgeport, Conn. 06603
IN OHIO
  141 West Rayen Ave.
    Youngstown, Ohio 44503
  Daughters of St. Paul
    Cleveland, Ohio
IN TEXAS
  114 East Main Plaza
    San Antonio, Texas 78205
IN CALIFORNIA
  1570 Fifth Ave.
    San Diego, Calif. 92101
  278 - 17th Street
    Oakland, California 94612
IN LOUISIANA
  86 Bolton Ave.
    Alexandria, La. 71303
IN FLORIDA
  2700 Biscayne Blvd.
    Miami, Florida 33137
IN CANADA
  8885 Blvd. Lacordaire
    St. Leonard Deport-Maurice
    Montreal, Canada
    1063 St. Clair Ave. West
    Toronto Canada
IN ENGLAND
  29 Beauchamp Place
    London, S.W. 3, England
IN AFRICA
  Box 4392
    Kampala, Uganda
IN INDIA
  Water Field Road Extension
  Plot No. 143
    Bandra, India
IN THE PHILIPPINE ISLANDS
  2650 F.B. Harrison St.
  Pasay City
    Philippine Islands
IN AUSTRALIA
  58 Abbotsford Rd.
    Homebush N.S.W., Australia
  226 Victoria Square
    Adelaide, South-Australia
  6 Muir Street
    Hawthorn, Victoria, Australia